NOT JUST A
LOAD OF OLD LENTILS

Rose Elliot became a cookery writer by accident. She was planning to take a history degree when she met and married her husband and became involved in cooking, entertaining and having babies. It was while looking after the latter that she began scribbling down her recipes. These led to her first book, *Simply Delicious*, which in turn brought requests for cookery demonstrations. It was the invention of new ideas and recipes for these that provided the impetus for *Not Just a Load of Old Lentils*. All her recipes are tried out on her family, who lament that they only get a dish while it's being tested: once it's right (and they like it) it goes into a book – and she starts trying out something else!

As well as writing regularly in the leading vegetarian newspaper *The Vegetarian*, Rose Elliot broadcasts and appears on television. She is actively involved in the work of The White Eagle Lodge, a religious charity concerned with the spiritual values of life, meditation and spiritual healing. Its philosophy seeks to show how every individual can help to alleviate suffering and improve conditions around him.

Not Just a Load of Old Lentils

ROSE ELLIOT

FONTANA/COLLINS

First published in Great Britain by
The White Eagle Publishing Trust 1972
Reprinted 1973
First issued in Fontana Books 1976
Second Impression June 1976
Third Impression January 1977
Fourth Impression July 1977
Fifth Impression January 1978
© Copyright Rose Elliot 1972

Made and printed in Great Britain by
William Collins Sons & Co Ltd

ACKNOWLEDGEMENTS

I am grateful to the many people who
have helped and encouraged me over this
book. I would especially like to thank
Ylana Hayward and Alison Innes for
their hours of patient work on the manu-
script and proofs; Geoffrey Dent for his
advice on wine; and 'Coralie' for her
careful testing of recipes.

CONTENTS

CONTENTS

PREFACE

Vegetarian cookery has a lot more to offer than dreary nut cutlets or lentil hotpot. In fact it is a whole new world of mouthwatering and delectable dishes for all occasions; soups, delicate and hearty, creamy and clear, piping hot or iced; salads and starters from a whole range of fruits and vegetables, from avocados and apples to fennel, leeks, sweetcorn and tomatoes; delicious vegetarian dips, mousses, timbales and pâtés; cooked dishes which range from vegetarian classics such as fondue, gnocchi, pipérade and oeufs florentine to stuffed aubergines, paëlla, chinese fried rice, and pepper and chestnut casserole, to mention only a few in the savouries section which covers all tastes, pockets and occasions. Equally delectable are the desserts, from the simple and fresh to the 'let's-celebrate-and-never-mind-the-calories' type. In fact, one could live for months on such a range of delicious and colourful dishes and hardly notice the fact that one had given up meat . . . except for an increase in health and vitality and a decrease in foodbills.

Meat-eaters will find many new ideas for bringing variety to their diet and for those occasions when they have vegetarians to entertain and want to offer something more than an omelette, while for vegetarians, this book contains many new and original ideas for practical, delicious and healthy meals.

I

I'D LIKE TO BE A VEGETARIAN, BUT ...

When people ask what a vegetarian eats, it's really very difficult to tell them in a few words. 'Well, we have nuts and lentils instead of meat, and of course there are lots of vegetables . . .' sounds awfully tame and about as interesting as a dry crust, and conveys nothing of the delicious, colourful mixtures of vegetables, fruits, rice – yes, and lentils – which we enjoy. The best way is to invite friends round to a meal and show them; or to give a cookery demonstration, and then they'll invariably say that they had no idea that vegetarian cookery was like *this*! I hope that this cookbook will fulfil a similar role to the cookery demonstration or dinner party in showing the variety and delectability of our food. Many of the recipes have been tried out on and approved by meat-eaters as well as by convinced vegetarians, and some are also ones I have used at demonstrations. After you've tried one or two of them you may feel, as people often do, 'I'd like to be a vegetarian, but . . .' and if this is the case, which I hope it is, then all I can say is please read on, and I hope you will find your reservations answered and will continue to enjoy the variety, flavour and economy of vegetarian recipes.

1. *Is it logical just to give up meat – shouldn't you give up milk and eggs, too?*

No, it isn't entirely logical because for instance, the milk industry is closely tied up with veal production with all its attendant cruelties.

But the fight against cruelty and bloodshed has to start somewhere. It's no good shrugging one's shoulders

1

and doing nothing because a system isn't perfect. Giving up the products of the slaughterhouse is a first step, and to take even that step is not easy for many people. However, once adapted to this new way of life, the vegetarian can begin using a plant-milk (Plamil is very good and is obtainable from health shops) instead of dairy milk and cream, and vegetable margarine instead of butter. For those who wish to take this extra step, I have included recipes for a plant-milk yoghurt and a plant-milk cottage cheese.

As far as eggs are concerned, if these are 'free range' – and it is a big 'if' – I do not personally see why, used sparingly, these are wrong. They are little more than 'seeds' at this stage, and involve no cruelty or exploitation. However, battery produced eggs are an entirely different matter, for the cruelty entailed in their production renders them unjustifiable, and if they were the only eggs available I should prefer to omit them altogether. Research has shown, incidentally, that such eggs are not as rich in vitamin B_{12} as naturally produced free range eggs. These latter are not always easy to obtain and unfortunately one can be misled over them. It is important to make thorough enquiries, insisting on *free* range, if you want to be sure. The euphemistic 'farm fresh' or 'fresh farm eggs' by no means denotes free range.

I see the ideal as being the gradual adoption of a humane vegetarian diet, the cutting out, first of all, of the slaughterhouse meats, followed by fish and fowl, and then the more and more frequent use of plant-milks to replace dairy foods. Softly, softly . . .

2. *If everyone becomes a vegetarian what will happen to all the animals? Surely they'll run wild/become extinct . . . ?*

At the moment animals are bred purely for slaughter. As more and more people become vegetarian, the breeders will simply breed fewer animals. It seems unlikely that thousands and thousands of people would become vegetarian overnight, so the decline of the meat industry would presumably be gradual. There certainly wouldn't be herds of wild bulls and boars running about! One would hope however that some small, regulated herds would be kept in farmlands, rather along the lines of herds of deer in National Parks.

3. *Will I get all the nourishment I need?*

Yes – and the chances are you'll feel fitter as well. Many nutritionists consider a vegetarian diet to be the best for health, and a balanced vegetarian diet can provide all the essential nutrients.

Carbohydrates for heat and energy are found in sugars and starchy foods, as in a meat diet. *Fats* which are used with carbohydrates to provide heat and energy are found in butter, also in the vegetable fats and oils used in the vegetarian diet to replace lard, dripping and animal-based margarine and cooking fats. *Protein* requirements, essential for growth and repair, can also be fully met on a vegetarian diet. Latest research indicates much lower daily intake than that previously considered necessary – an average of around 40 grammes of protein a day. (See Table 1, Recommended Intakes of Energy and Nutrients for the U.K. (1969) published by the Department of Health and Social Security.) This can easily be obtained by taking, say, a pint of milk and 2 oz. of cheese; or half a pint of milk, 1 oz. of cheese, a large egg, and three good slices of bread. Foods from which protein is derived in the vegetarian diet are: milk, eggs, nuts, pulses and the new soya proteins; and if a good source of protein is included at each meal as in the recipes in this book, the requirements can be more than adequately met.

Incidentally, modern research has dismissed the conception of proteins as being 'first class' and 'second class': vegetable and animal proteins are used together in the body to provide the full range of amino acids essential for health.

Vitamin and mineral requirements too are well covered in a balanced vegetarian diet; rich sources of vitamin A for growth and resistance to disease are butter and margarine, milk, eggs, carrots, dark green leafy vegetables, tomatoes, dried apricots and figs. A good serving of green vegetables, or perhaps dried apricots or figs for breakfast, and the use of vegetable margarine or butter, cheese and eggs, ensures adequate amounts. Vitamin B is composed of a number of different constituents, the most important being *thiamine*, *riboflavin* and *niacin* or *nicotinic acid*. They are very important for proper muscular activity, the utilisation of carbohydrates, and functioning of the nervous system. *Thiamine* is found in brazilnuts, peanuts, oatmeal, soya flour, wholemeal flour and bread, brewers' yeast powder, yeast extracts and peas. Frequent use of oatmeal, perhaps in the form of muesli, also wholemeal bread and flour, and generous use of yeast extracts, will ensure an adequate supply.

Riboflavin is obtained from milk and cheese, yoghurt, cottage cheese, brewers' yeast powder and yeast extracts, also in tea; while *niacin* or *nicotinic acid* is found in peanuts and peanut butter, wholemeal bread and brewers' yeast powder. B_{12} is found in cheese, milk and eggs, also in some of the new textured soya proteins, in comfrey (which Marigold market as a 'tea' and can be used as a basis for vegetable stocks) and dulse, also from Marigold. One of the easiest ways of ensuring adequate amounts of the B vitamins is to take powdered brewers' yeast. Brewers' yeast is a natural food (not a drug) and a wonderful source of the B vitamins as well as of iron. It can be taken in its powdered form, two dessertspoonfuls stirred into a glass of orange juice, or in tablets; if you are taking it in its powdered form, start with a bare half teaspoonful and *gradually* increase to the full amount. The frequent use of yeast extracts for cooking, sensible helpings of milk (or for vegans, vitamin enriched plant-milk), eggs and cheese (for vegans, soya flour and sesame seeds and spreads) wholemeal bread and cereals, also nuts, and, particularly for children, peanuts and peanut butter, will ensure that the daily requirements of B vitamins are adequately met.

Vitamin C, for vitality, building and mending tissues, is found in fresh fruit (particularly blackcurrants and oranges) and vegetables, such as sprouts, cabbage, cauliflower, watercress, peppers, potato and lettuce. An orange a day, or a glass of orange juice is a good idea, and good servings of fresh vegetables. Vegetarians can get sufficient vitamin D, which controls absorption of calcium and phosphorus necessary for healthy bones and teeth, from eggs and margarine. It is also absorbed by the action of sunlight on the skin. Extra vitamin D for children can be given in the form of drops of synthetic vitamin D, called Adexolin.

As for the essential *minerals*, in this country there is little danger of shortage of copper, iodine, sodium, potassium and phosphorus. *Iodine* can be provided by the use of agar agar to make moulds and jellies; it is present in some soils, so vegetables grown in iodine rich areas contain it. *Calcium*, necessary for strong teeth, bones and proper functioning of blood, is found in milk, cheese, eggs, almonds, brazilnuts, cabbage, broccoli, watercress, wholemeal bread, potato, soya flour, dried apricots and oatmeal. *Iron* for healthy blood and vitality is present in eggs, pulses such as baked beans, soya beans and soya flour and lentils, wholemeal flour and bread, wheat germ, oatmeal, yeast and yeast products such as marmite, yeastrel; black treacle, cocoa and plain chocolate; nuts (almonds, brazilnuts, cashews, hazelnuts, walnuts), dried fruits (apricots, figs, raisins and dates), potatoes and leafy green vegetables and watercress.

In a well-balanced vegetarian diet there is little danger of any serious deficiency occurring. It is important however, in any diet, to look to the natural foods so rich in nourishment and see that these are used before the other fancy, refined foods.

4. Will I have to use lots of expensive 'health foods'?

A vegetarian diet is simply one which avoids the flesh of slaughtered animals, and certainly need not include 'lots of fancy health foods'. But there are certain foods which make sense to use in any diet. All the nourishment we need for perfect health is contained within the fruits of the earth. In its natural form the food is perfectly balanced to give us the various nutrients in their right proportions, the different parts acting and interacting on each other. Take bread, for example; a grain of corn consists of three parts, the heart or germ, the starch and the bran. Nearly all the vitamins and minerals are contained in the heart or germ and the bran. Yet in the process of making white flour these are removed, being 'replaced' by added vitamins, often in the wrong proportions. I know people say, because of this, white flour is richer than brown in calcium and other nutrients – but not in the right, natural proportions. Then take sugar. In its natural form, sugar is wrapped up in very bulky fruits and vegetables; sugar cane, sugar beet, fruits. To get a little sugar from these requires an awful lot of chewing! Thus, in its natural form there is a limit to the amount of sugar we can eat. However, with modern refining methods, sugar is readily available in very pleasant, easy-to-take forms, such as sweets, ice-cream, cakes, drinks and so on. Sugar has therefore become one of the scourges of the present day, resulting in obesity, tooth decay and having serious association with heart disease and other modern illnesses. So it surely makes good sense, to my mind anyway, to limit the intake of sugar, having fresh or dried fruit instead of too many sweet puddings and cakes, fruit juices instead of sweetened drinks. Where sweetening is required, the use of honey or the more natural dark brown barbados sugar is strongly recommended.

There is no need to use gimmicky health foods; just the natural, unrefined foods which are our right. What we eat is largely habit, and if we can get used to using the healthier, whole foods (while not becoming fanatical) I'm sure it is all to the good. Intelligent use of whole foods is one thing, grim-faced fanaticism is quite another, and such an attitude has no place in a balanced happy life.

Most of the ingredients used in this book are easily obtainable. In fact, although I live in the country I have been able to buy all the items in our local town and village shops, but if you have any difficulty, I hope the section 'Where to buy . . .' at the end of the book will help.

As a footnote I would like to mention that an example of what can be achieved by living on natural foods is provided by the Hunzas. This race of people was discovered in 1936 living in the Himalayas. Because the country is so inaccessible their way of life has been unchanged by civilisation. Their diet still consists of food in its natural form, most of it raw. They live fairly sparsely on whole cereals, nuts, fruits and vegetables, with a little goat's milk and honey. All who have seen these people report on the beauty and excellence of their physique. Obesity and disease are unknown, as are crime and violence. Men play polo at 70 years of age, and men of 90 and 100 think nothing of walking 10 or 12 miles, the life expectancy being about 120 years.

5. *Isn't it expensive . . . all those nuts?*

No – and all *what* nuts? A glance through this book will, I think, show that we don't eat nuts in the vast quantities many people imagine! But let's analyse the diet. The main difference between a meat diet and a vegetarian diet is the protein; while a vegetarian depends entirely on vegetable and dairy sources of protein, a meat-eater uses these combined with meat and fish. A vegetarian would probably spend more on cheese, on pulses such as lentils, soya protein and on nuts. Of these the latter are the most expensive item, but 8 oz. of nuts made into one of our savouries would feed 4–6 people very well. The equivalent in meat could not cost less than double the price of the nuts. We might spend more on vegetables, and of course on wholemeal flour and bread, natural rice and sugar which most of us use, but generally speaking most people find they can live more cheaply on a vegetarian diet, even allowing for this.

Here are some examples of inexpensive vegetarian main courses:

Ratatouille with crusty bread rolls and grated cheese; tossed green salad and cooked peas

Sweetcorn fritters with tomato sauce; spinach, sauté potatoes, braised onions

Cauliflower à la polonaise; buttered cabbage, finger carrots

Mushroom stuffed pancakes; vegetables in season

6. *Will I have to buy lots of new equipment?*

No; the equipment needed for vegetarian cookery is usually to be found in an ordinary kitchen. An electric grater such as a moulinex is helpful but not essential for grating up nuts and salads. I have also found one of those round spring choppers, such as the maxichop, useful. A few bangs on this and a whole pile of nuts is very finely chopped, also cabbage, onions and other vegetables can be shredded in this way. A pressure cooker is useful for making speedy meals, especially some of the thick meal-in-one-pan soups in Chapter II. A liquidiser or mouli légumes is very useful for soup making.

7. *I haven't time . . .*

Preparing vegetarian meals is a new art to most people; it may take a little longer at first because the methods and ingredients are unfamiliar. One has to allow for this; so choose quick meals to start with and plan a little more carefully. I do not believe that our meals take any longer to cook once one is used to the methods. The time-consuming part of cooking is in thinking *what* to cook, and much time can be saved by sitting down once a week, or even once a fortnight, recipe book in hand, to plan the main dish for each day of the given period. All the main shopping can then be done in one operation – and here we *do* save time as vegetarians for our proteins keep so well that we really can shop for them once a week, once a fortnight or less. The Index/Menu-Planner will, I hope, help to make the planning quick and easy. For those days when the organisation has gone awry, or when there's very little time for cooking, I've listed easy meals under 'quick family meals' and 'quick entertaining' in the Index/Menu-Planner. Here is a sample of some quick menus:

Fondue with crusty french bread; tossed green salad; fresh fruit

Egg and mushroom pilau; watercress or green salad; bananas with chocolate sauce.

Pipérade with crusty rolls; green salad or cooked broccoli; fresh fruit

Courgettes mornay or celery hearts mornay; peas, braised tomatoes; muesli

8. *Isn't it a job to get enough variety?*

To be honest, I think a vegetarian does need to think a little harder about menus, and maybe use more imagination and inventive power. But in this book alone there are over 400 recipes, so variety can't be too limited, even allowing that the ingredients for some of the recipes will be out of season at any one time, and some are for special occasions. No, with the number of vegetables and exciting foods now available, variety really isn't a problem.

I would like to add that although many people raise this question about variety, surveys have shown that in fact the majority of meat-eaters do live on a very limited range of foods and menus. Perhaps there is room in many meat-eaters' diets for some vegetarian dishes to bring more interest. A meat-eating friend who tested many of the recipes for me was quite amazed at how much *more* variety there is in the vegetarian diet and told me the other day it had quite transformed her attitude to cooking.

9. *Isn't it very fattening?*

A properly balanced vegetarian diet is no more fattening than a meat one. Consider, for instance, the number of slender models and film stars who are vegetarians! Once you are at your proper weight, you can stay there by being sensible about diet, just as you can on a meat diet.

In this matter of slimming, mental attitude is all-important. So often people will go on a crash diet and lose weight, and then immediately revert to old eating habits and swiftly put it all on again. Or, having been extremely strict and self-denying, their body will suddenly rebel and they will break away from the discipline of the diet in a weak moment, and then feel that all is lost and they might as well give up. These failures occur largely because of the concept of a temporary, special slimming diet, followed by a 'normal diet' which is again followed in a few months' time by another slimming diet involving further effort of will.

Instead of this, I think one has really got to get to grips

with the situation and decide whether one wants to spend one's life going from one diet to another, or whether one wants to find a way of life which eliminates that need. This latter is perfectly possible, and here's how.

First of all, stop thinking that you're about to go on a diet. Think instead of a new, healthy and slim way of life. No more worries over added inches, no more feelings of guilt and remorse. Too good to be true? Well, it does involve some initial discipline, but because this way of eating is adapted to your own needs and way of life, it should not be too difficult to follow. If you have weight to lose, start this eating-plan, allowing yourself 1,000 calories a day which will result in a loss of 1 to 2 lbs. a week. As the pounds roll away you can fill out this eating-plan quite naturally by keeping its basic structure but allowing more scope with savouries.

If you like tea and coffee with milk, allow ½ pint a day and write down 190 calories for this straight away. At first, measure out your day's supply into a special jug to keep it separate from the rest of the family's. After a little while you will instinctively know how much you use during a day and will not need to measure specially.

I know many diets tell us to start with a good breakfast; but again, being a non-good-breakfaster myself I do sympathise with those who find this difficult! So, in order to make a harmonious eating-plan, I suggest here you adapt to your own needs, having for instance one of the following, accordingly:

¼ pint natural yoghurt, and a piece of wholemeal toast with a scraping of butter

approx. 200 calories

or

1 oz. all-bran or other cereal, with milk from daily allowance; piece of wholemeal toast, as above

approx. 200 calories
(excluding milk which is counted separately)

or
1 orange and a piece of wholemeal toast, as above

approx. 175 calories

or
1 boiled egg and a piece of wholemeal toast, as above

approx. 180 calories

Coffee or tea as required, with milk from daily allowance; take no sugar in either, but saccharin if you like. Try, however, to cut down on this, in order to educate your palate to a healthier way of life.

A cup of tea or coffee at mid-day if liked – or water or fruit juice. Allow about 45 calories for a small glass of fruit juice.

I think it is best to make one meal a day very simple indeed, and to keep it like this. It can be the evening meal if you like, but personally I prefer to make it lunch. But decide whichever fits in best with your routine and try to have a simple salad (about 50–100 calories) with a little cottage cheese (70 calories for 2 ozs.) or 1 oz. of cheese (90–120 calories), or a hardboiled egg (80 calories) followed by an apple or pear (50 calories) or orange (75 calories). Make the salad as interesting as you like, using ideas in this book, but avoid oil in dressings – use lemon juice, cider vinegar or a little yoghurt instead.

At tea-time, it is best to get into the habit of just a drink – tea, coffee or fruit juice. But for those times when you feel that tired, sinking feeling, have a teaspoonful of honey (about 16 calories) or an orange or apple; and if possible, get away from the kitchen and put your feet up for a few minutes until the feeling passes!

The evening meal, or main meal of the day, should consist of plenty of cooked vegetables – one of these to be a green, leafy one – at least two generous helpings (but not peas or baked beans). Allow about 50 calories a serving of vegetables. Have these with a small portion of savoury from this book, but cook the savouries carefully while you are actually trying to lose weight, using as little fat and flour as possible, and cutting down on other starchy ingredients within the recipes. You will find some of the textured vegetable protein recipes useful; also such dishes as cheese soufflés, stuffed eggs, vegetable mornay. For a simple cooked meal, have a medium-sized baked potato (90 calories) with 1 oz. of grated cheese or some cottage cheese. Instead of gravy and sauces, use a little tomato juice, or have a fresh juicy tomato with your meal. Finish with an apple, orange, half a banana or a few grapes.

You can keep to this eating-plan for as long as you like, or until you have achieved your correct weight. Then, simply increase the amount and types of savouries you have in the cooked meal, and add a medium-sized potato when the meal doesn't include lentils, rice, pastry or breadcrumbs. Finish sometimes with fresh fruit, sometimes with one of the light, fruity desserts in this book. Also, have a little soup with your light meal if you like, but apart from this, try to keep to this basic framework of healthy eating, and I hope you will find you do not have to diet again.

Of course there are times when the diet has to slip – a special meal, or Christmas time, for example; but it is your basic, everyday diet which determines whether you are fat or thin, and after a celebration meal you can always have a light day's eating with a very simple savoury in the main meal.

Watch the scales, for the great thing is not to let over-weight get the upper hand; it is not difficult to shed three pounds – but three pounds can soon become half a stone, then a stone and in no time, a stone and a half. And to lose a stone and a half demands a major effort of will power. Only *you* can cope with the problem; and only *you* will know how much better you feel when you get to your right weight – and in the achievement of this the vegetarian diet will help rather than hinder you, if planned intelligently.

10. *Will it satisfy my family?*

Hearty, filling family meals can certainly be provided by a vegetarian diet, as I am sure a glance through this book will show. Many children are natural vegetarians, and will only eat meat when encouraged or even coerced. Here is a sample of menus for good family meals:

Fried gnocchi with parsley sauce; cabbage; grilled tomatoes; chips; apricot fool

Mixed vegetable curry with rice; tossed green salad; real pineapple jelly

Mushroom timbale with sauce espagnole (brown sauce); greens; sliced carrots; sauté potatoes; rosy apples

Mixed grill; tossed side salad; bakewell tart

Mushroom pie; mashed potato; vegetables in season; muesli

11. *I live on my own . . . .*

Then you're in a perfect position for changing your diet, and one advantage about the vegetarian diet is that you don't have the embarrassment of asking for tiny portions of meat and fish. You can buy 1 lb. of nuts or lentils or soya protein like everyone else, and know they will keep.

Obviously things like omelettes are easiest; and an omelette and tossed salad or toasted cheese and a salad, or crusty bread, cheese and fruit, contains as much nourishment as a cooked meal – more than a badly planned meal such as chips, fish fingers and peas. But those living on their own need variety as much as anyone else. Many of the recipes in this book can be scaled down for one person, or, half the quantity given in the recipe can be used and the savoury used for two days' needs. Here are some ideas:

Gnocchi – make half the quantity, for two days, frying the gnocchi the second day. Serve with tomato sauce and watercress

Pipérade – make a quarter of the quantity given. Eat with crusty roll and green salad

Fondue – very easy to make – make quarter of quantity given. Again serve with crusty roll and tossed green salad

Stuffed pancakes – make a batch to keep in a plastic box in the fridge and use as required with mushrooms or tomato and cheese to stuff them

Lentils and mushrooms au gratin – make half quantity for two meals; the second day make into fritters and serve with lemon slices, brown sauce (which will keep for a fortnight in the fridge) and vegetables

Paëlla or egg and pea pilau – make half quantity, for two days, using remains on the second day to stuff a pepper, courgette or aubergine

Chop suey – any of the varieties given – make quarter of the quantity given. Serve with omelette shreds or toasted almonds (which can be kept in a tin to use as required)

Mushroom savoury – make quarter quantity

12. *I have to eat out such a lot . . .*

Fortunately the number of good vegetarian restaurants and fresh juice bars is increasing almost weekly, and if there is one of these at hand the problem is solved. It is also possible to get a completely vegetarian meal in many Indian restaurants, since many Indians are by religion vegetarian. When neither of these possibilities is available, one usually has to resort to the inevitable omelette or cheese salad, which does not really make for interest. This is a pity, because there are so many other delicious vegetarian savouries which would not be difficult for caterers to prepare: vegetarian pizzas, paëllas, stuffed vegetables, quiches, fondue, gnocchi – to mention only a few. Let us hope that some of these will begin to appear on the menus of ordinary restaurants, together with some of the more exciting salads and starters such as those given in Chapter III.

Where friends are concerned, obviously it can be a nuisance for a hostess to have to make something special for a vegetarian. Advance warning is of course only polite, and if necessary, just eating the vegetables without the main course. But in our experience many hostesses really enjoy the challenge of creating a vegetarian dish – providing they are given plenty of warning. If you want to give up meat, like giving up smoking, you've got to take your courage in both hands and firmly announce that this is what you have done. You may even convert your friends eventually! I hope this book will be helpful to hostesses with vegetarians to feed.

13. *What about entertaining?* . . .

In my experience most people are at first slightly apprehensive, maybe intrigued, and later delighted, when offered a vegetarian meal, and conversions are not unknown after one or two good meals.

Even today, so many people still have the old-fashioned image of vegetarian fare consisting of a hard nut cutlet and limp lettuce leaf, eaten with grim-faced determination, that it's fun to disillusion them with real vegetarian food. In this book there are many special dishes suitable for entertaining. To give you an idea of some typical meals, here are some examples of what a vegetarian can eat on high days and holidays. For a special lunch or informal late supper, for instance, how do you feel about:

Cream of corn soup; asparagus soufflé quiche; avocado and mushroom salad followed by ratafia cream

For summer, what about:

Gazpacho, followed by mixed fruit salad with cottage cheese dressing, with pineapple and grape compôte to follow and some nice coffee with cream

For a dinner party, maybe one of these three menus, made up from recipes taken at random from the book, would be acceptable:

Egg and avocado pâté; stuffed aubergines provençales; duchesse potatoes; sauce espagnole; celery hearts; buttered spinach; zabaglione

Aubergine and tomato salad; paëlla with lemon sauce; french beans; braised tomatoes; special chocolate icecream

Leeks vinaigrette; mushroom soufflé; croquette potatoes; finger carrots; buttered broccoli spears; peach and raspberry layer

Many different party menus, too, can be made up from the recipes – here's just one example:

Aubergine and rice salad; chaudfroid of asparagus; artichoke heart salad; cucumber and yoghurt salad; salted nuts; cheese board; french bread; chestnut meringue gâteau or black forest gâteau or stuffed peaches

14. *I like a little wine sometimes . . .*

And you can have it – why not? Wine goes beautifully with nearly all vegetarian dishes – indeed two important ingredients of vegetarian food, cheese and nuts, are often cited in wine books as being the ideal partners for wine. These same wine books, however, ignore vegetarian dishes; if there is a wine expert who is also a vegetarian he has kept very quiet about it! I am therefore including some notes of possible wines to drink with these recipes. These are not notes by wine experts but by my family and friends and are made to start you off. The important thing about wine is to enjoy it – don't forget to admire the colour and fragrance of a wine – and it is a good idea to experiment with different wines and foods to discover which combinations you prefer. If you do not know much about wine, you might like to read one of the excellent short introductory books that are available.* (If you know a lot about wine you won't need these ideas anyway!)

The various main dishes are taken in the same order as the recipes in Chapter IV and the suggestions as to the wine to go with them are not meant to be exhaustive. In vegetarian cooking the main ingredient in a dish may for example be cheese, or nuts, each of which has a distinctive flavour of its own, but the many and varied other items in the dish can quite change the final flavour and thus influence the choice of wine to match it. In general we find that the stronger wines (and more often the red wines) seem to blend particularly well with the stronger dishes, and that the lighter wines (particularly the white wines) often go best with the milder food.

* For example, *The Plain Man's Guide to Wine*, by Raymond Postgate (Joseph).

EGG DISHES

The basic egg flavour tends to swamp a delicate wine, and the richer red wines of the Rhône or Burgundy and the Spanish wines of similar type are suggested here. Chianti, Valpolicella and other Italian wines go well with most egg dishes, particularly with the strong flavoured pipérade.

CHEESE DISHES

Cheese on its own goes excellently with most wines – with the strong cheeses such as blue stilton which traditionally end the meal, take a strong wine like Port or Madeira; but if you save a little of the table wines of your choice to accompany the cheese you should be well rewarded. Dry white wines go very well with cheese and cheese dishes – the classic accompaniment to fondue is a dry Swiss white wine.

GNOCCHI, PASTA, PIZZA

With these traditional Italian meals, why not drink a traditional Italian wine? Chianti or Frascati are two possibilities.

The recipe for gnocchi is mild and would go well with hock or most French or Spanish white wines or rosé. The pasta dishes will go with most wines and as their flavourings vary greatly it is a good idea to experiment and see what you like.

QUICHE

The most famous quiche of Lorraine is often accompanied by the dry white wines of Moselle and Alsace, so why not try some with the quiches listed here? Rosé and other white wines would also go well with them.

19

CURRY

Curry kills the flavour of wine so don't drink wine with it – try lager, ginger beer or fruit juice. (If you doubt this, try an experiment: the next time you have curry taste the wine before you eat any and then again afterwards.)

PAËLLA, VEGETABLE DISHES, PROTOVEG DISHES

Try the delicate white wines with the asparagus mornay and other mild dishes. Aubergines provençales, the croustades and other strong dishes match with the stronger red Rhône or Burgundy wines or the Spanish wines of a similar type.

NUT DISHES

Nuts by themselves go excellently with sherry as an apéritif or Madeira to end the meal, but when cooked, most nut dishes have strong flavours requiring red or white Burgundy, Rhône or similar wines. An exception is the delicate nut meat made from cashews or almonds where a rosé or dry white wine would be very pleasant.

WINE IN COOKING

Don't overlook the use of wine in cooking, where it can give an unusual and attractive flavour. The secret of wine cooking is the same as the secret of using herbs – restraint. Your guests should wonder what is giving the subtle flavouring to a dish, rather than recognising at once what you have done. The following are brief suggestions as to how wine can effectively be used in cooking. (The easiest way of getting wine for cooking is to save the undrunk remains in bottles. If you do buy wine specially for cooking buy the cheapest you can – once cooked there is no difference between that and the most expensive wines.)

Soup

A tablespoon of wine or sherry added in the bowl just before serving soup is effective, particularly with mushroom or tomato soup.

Main Dishes

Try adding a little wine or sherry to nearly any of the main dishes in Chapter IV of this book. Whether absorbed in the filling of a quiche, pancake or timbale or added to a croquette, croustade or rice dish, the result can be appetising and unusual.

Vegetables

Have you ever tried red wine added to red cabbage or baked beans? How about mushrooms simmered in wine and cabbage or carrots cooked in Sauterne? An exotic vegetable can surprise your guests!

Sweets

The sweeter wines – Hock or Sauterne – go well with fruit and fruit dishes, as does Kirsch – several of the recipes have them included.

I hope, whether you're a vegetarian or not, you'll enjoy the recipes in this book, and also find it useful when entertaining vegetarian friends and visitors.

Unless otherwise stated, quantities given serve from 4 to 5 people.

II

SOUPS – QUICK AND EASY

Soups really *are* quick and easy to make, and vegetarian soups particularly so, as they take only as long to
cook as the vegetables from which they're made, about
thirty-five minutes altogether depending on the vegetables used; and the smaller the vegetables are cut, the
sooner the soup will be ready. A pressure cooker of
course cuts the cooking time by two-thirds and brings
soups into the 'emergency meal' category. In fact the
heartier soups in this chapter make excellent meals in
themselves, a good bowlful served with a tossed green
salad and grated cheese or a cheese board and crusty
bread. A meal like this is most nourishing and wel-
coming – economical, too, both of money and time and
easy on the washing up afterwards. For more formal
occasions, soups can be prettied up in many simple ways,
and I have listed some ideas for quick garnishes at the
end of the chapter.

In all these recipes 'stock' means the liquor strained
from cooked vegetables (containing so much of the
goodness, too) or water in which a vegetarian stock cube
(from health food stores) has been dissolved. Failing
either of these, water can be used, but in this case the
soup will need extra careful seasoning.

As with sauces, it is best to use 81 per cent rather than
100 per cent wholemeal flour to thicken soups when
necessary as the former is more glutinous and usually
preferable flavourwise and nutritionally to cornflour,
although sometimes cornflour is used for the sake of
appearance.

Clear Soups

Clear Asparagus Soup

1 small onion
½ oz. butter
10½ oz. can chopped
  green asparagus
water – see recipe

2 tsp. cornflour
1 tbs. finely chopped
  parsley
salt and pepper
dash of lemon juice

Peel and finely slice onion; sauté for 10 minutes in the butter, but do not brown. Drain asparagus, making liquor up to 1½ pints with water, and mixing with the cornflour, then add to onion with chopped parsley. Simmer for 15 minutes. Season with salt, lemon juice, and a very little pepper.

This soup is also delicious served chilled with a slice of lemon in each bowl – but in this case use vegetable oil instead of the butter.

Clear Celery Soup

½ head celery
1 onion
1 desstsp. vegetable oil
½ tsp. celery salt

1¾ pints water or stock
1 tsp. yeast extract
2 tbs. finely chopped
  celery leaves

Wash and fairly finely slice celery and onion. Sauté in the oil for 5 minutes, but do not brown. Add celery salt, water and yeast extract, and simmer for 30–40 minutes. Check seasoning. Add finely chopped celery leaves.

Clear Mushroom Soup

2 medium onions
½ lb. mushrooms or
  mushroom stalks
bouquet garni – bayleaf,
  sprig thyme, bunch
  parsley stalks, sprig
  chervil, tied together

½ oz. butter
1¾ pints water or stock
1 tsp. yeast extract
salt and pepper
2 heaped tbs. chopped
  parsley

23

Slice onion; chop mushrooms or mushroom stalks, washed but unpeeled. Sauté onion and mushroom together in the butter for 5 minutes without browning. Add the bouquet garni, water and yeast extract, and simmer for 30 minutes. Remove bouquet garni. Season with salt and pepper. Serve with a good sprinkling of chopped parsley on each bowl.

Clear Vegetable Soup

2 sticks celery	1 tsp. yeast extract
2 onions	1 tsp. tomato purée
2 carrots	1 bayleaf
other vegetables as available; a little chopped cabbage, a few french beans	$1\frac{1}{2}$ pints water or stock salt and freshly ground black pepper
$\frac{1}{2}$ tbs. vegetable oil	2 tbs. chopped fresh chives

Slice celery; peel and slice onions and carrots. Sauté together in the oil without browning for 5 minutes. Break beans into short lengths; shred cabbage, and add. Toss over a gentle heat for a further 5 minutes. Add yeast extract, tomato purée, bayleaf and water, and simmer for 20–30 minutes. Season with salt and freshly ground black pepper. Sprinkle with the chopped chives. Serve very hot with croûtons.

Other combinations of vegetables can of course be used, aiming for variety in colour and flavour.

THICK AND CREAM SOUPS

Cream of Artichoke Soup

1 lb. jerusalem artichokes	¾ pint water or white stock
1 tbs. vinegar	salt and pepper
1 onion	grated nutmeg
1 tbs. vegetable oil	squeeze of lemon juice
¾ pint milk	croûtons to serve
	small carton single cream (optional)

Peel artichokes, tiny 'lumps' and all. Cut roughly, and place straight into cold water to which 1 tbs. vinegar has been added – this helps preserve colour. Slice onion and sauté in the oil for 5 minutes; add sliced and drained artichokes and cook for a further 5 minutes, before pouring in the milk and water, and simmering until artichokes are soft, about 30 minutes. Sieve or liquidise; correct seasoning, add nutmeg and a squeeze of lemon juice to taste. Serve with a garnish of crisp croûtons.

This is a rather special, delicately flavoured soup which is enhanced, when budget allows, by the addition of a small carton of single cream just before serving.

Cream of Asparagus Soup

10½ oz. can asparagus	1 oz. butter
¾ pint water approx.	2 heaped tbs. flour
½ pint milk approx.	salt and pepper
1 onion	chopped parsley and lemon slices to garnish
piece lemon rind	
3 sprigs parsley	

Drain liquid from asparagus and make up to 1½ pints with milk and water. Chop asparagus. Bring liquid to boiling point in a pan with onion and lemon rind and parsley, then remove from heat and leave for 10–15 minutes, then strain, discarding onion, lemon and parsley. Meanwhile melt butter in a pan – without browning; stir in flour and cook gently for 2 minutes, then remove from heat. Carefully stir in milk mixture; return to heat, add asparagus, stir till mixture thickens, then simmer gently for 15 minutes. Serve with a sprinkling of chopped parsley and a slice of lemon in each bowl.

Beetroot Soup

1 onion
1 large potato
3 tbs. vegetable oil
1 lb. cooked beetroot
1 piece pared lemon
  rind
1½ pints water or
  vegetable stock

salt and pepper
juice of ½ lemon
to serve: small carton fresh or
  soured cream
2 tbs. finely chopped
  chives or mint

Peel and chop onion and potato; sauté together in the oil for 5 minutes, then add the beetroot, roughly sliced, lemon rind and water; simmer for 20–30 minutes until potato is soft; liquidise and season to taste with salt, pepper and lemon juice. Reheat, ladle into bowls, then pour a little cream into each one, swirling it round attractively on the deep red soup. Finish with a scattering of fresh chopped chives or mint. A very pretty, refreshing soup which can also be served chilled.

Thick Butterbean and Tomato Soup

8 oz. butterbeans
1½ pints water or stock
2 large onions
1 bayleaf
1 oz. butter

15 oz. can tomatoes
piece lemon peel
salt, pepper and sugar to
  taste
raw onion circles to garnish

Soak butterbeans overnight in water. Next day measure water, and make up to 1½ pints. Slice onions and sauté with the bayleaf in the butter for 5 minutes. Add tomatoes, roughly sliced, and butterbeans with their water, lemon peel, salt, pepper and sugar. Simmer very gently for $1\frac{1}{2}$ to 2 hours until beans are tender. Check seasoning. Garnish with thin circles of onion.

This is a hearty, satisfying soup, and served with grated cheese and perhaps a tossed green salad makes a complete meal. If, instead of the dried butterbeans, two 15 oz. cans of butterbeans are used, this becomes a quickly made 'emergency' meal or a good quick supper.

Cream of Cabbage Soup

1 onion	$\frac{3}{4}$ pint water
1 large potato	$\frac{3}{4}$ pint milk
1 oz. butter	nutmeg
1 lb. cabbage	salt and pepper

Peel and slice onion and potato and sauté gently in the butter for 10 minutes. Meanwhile wash and shred cabbage and add to onion and potato and cook for a further 2–3 minutes. Add the water and simmer gently for 30 minutes or until potato is cooked, then add the milk and seasoning and reheat, but do not boil. Liquidise and season with nutmeg, salt and pepper.

An economical and nourishing soup.

Carrot and Lemon Soup

1 onion	$1\frac{1}{2}$ pints water or stock
2 sticks celery	salt
6 medium-sized carrots	freshly ground black
1 oz. butter	pepper
rind and juice of $\frac{1}{2}$ lemon	chopped parsley to serve
1 bayleaf	

Chop onion, celery and carrots fairly finely; sauté gently in the butter for 5–10 minutes until beginning to soften but not brown. Add half the thinly pared lemon rind, bayleaf and water, and simmer for about 45 minutes. Liquidise, add lemon juice to taste and the rest of the lemon rind, salt, and a discreet grating of freshly ground black pepper. Serve with a generous sprinkling of chopped parsley, or a touch of fresh marjoram, or thyme when available.

Cream of Cauliflower Soup

1 small cauliflower
1 small onion
small clove garlic
1 oz. butter
$\frac{3}{4}$ pint water or
    white stock

$\frac{3}{4}$ pint milk
$\frac{1}{2}$ pint single cream or top milk
salt and pepper
paprika and croûtons to garnish

Wash cauliflower and chop, discarding any discoloured or tough leaves. Peel and chop onion, crush garlic, sauté all together in the butter without browning for 5 minutes. Add water and milk mixed. Cover and simmer for 30 minutes. Liquidise all but two ladlefuls of soup – these give texture. Add cream and season carefully. Serve with a good sprinkling of paprika and a garnish of croûtons.

Celery and Tomato Soup

3 onions
outside stalks from
    1 head celery
1 tbs. vegetable oil
15 oz. can tomatoes
1 bayleaf

1 pint water or stock
salt
pepper
sugar
juice and rind of $\frac{1}{2}$ lemon
1 tbs. chopped celery leaves

Peel and chop onions; wash and slice celery, and sauté together in the oil without browning for 5–10 minutes. Add tomatoes, roughly chopped, bayleaf and water, and simmer for 30 minutes, until celery is tender.

Season well with salt, pepper and sugar, and a little lemon juice. Add chopped celery leaves, and serve each bowl garnished with pared lemon rind snipped into $\frac{1}{2}''$ slivers.

Variation: This soup is very good made with 1 or 2 diced celeriacs replacing the chopped celery.

Cream of Corn Soup

1 onion	paprika
1 oz. butter	dash of lemon juice
11½ oz. can sweetcorn	salt and pepper
1¼ pints water	slices of green pepper to
¼ pint single cream	garnish

Peel and chop onion and sauté without browning in the butter for 5 minutes. Add sweetcorn with its liquid and 1¼ pints water. Simmer for 30 minutes. Liquidise all but a good ladleful which is left to give texture, then stir in the cream, paprika and a little lemon juice, salt and pepper to taste.

For special occasions serve each bowl garnished with one or two very thin green pepper circles.

Dhal Soup

8 oz. red lentils	½ tsp. turmeric
1¾ pints water	2 tbs. oil
1 bayleaf	2 tsp. garam masala
2 medium onions, sliced	dash of lemon juice
2 cloves garlic, crushed	salt and pepper
½ tsp. ginger	lemon rings to serve

Soak lentils in the water overnight, or at least for a few hours, then simmer gently with the bayleaf, half the onions and half the garlic, the ginger and turmeric until tender – about half an hour. Meanwhile fry the rest of the onion and garlic in the oil until browned, add garam masala and pour into the lentils, oil and all. Stir and leave for at least 10 minutes for the flavours to blend – better if you can leave it longer. Season carefully and sharpen with a dash of lemon juice; reheat and garnish with lemon rings.

This is a thick, satisfying soup; a large, steaming bowlful of it on a winter's evening makes a complete meal, with a simple tossed salad and fruit.

Egg and Onion Soup

6 medium-sized onions	1 bayleaf
1 oz. butter	a little powdered mace
2 tbs. flour	salt and pepper
1¾ pints milk and water, mixed	4 hard-boiled eggs
	1 tbs. chopped parsley

Peel and chop onions; sauté gently in the butter without browning for 5 minutes; add flour, stir until blended, then gradually add the liquid. Simmer gently with a bayleaf for 15 minutes, then season with mace, salt and pepper. Add hard-boiled eggs, finely chopped, and heat through before serving, garnished with chopped parsley.

Golden Soup

1 onion	15 oz. can tomatoes
1 carrot	1 pint water or stock
1 oz. butter	rind and juice of ½ lemon
1 bayleaf	salt and pepper

Peel and chop onion; peel and coarsely grate carrot. Sauté both in the butter with the bayleaf for 10 minutes until slightly softened, but not browned. Add tomatoes, roughly chopped, water or stock, and pared lemon rind. Simmer gently for 30 minutes. Remove bayleaf. Liquidise two-thirds of soup. Add to rest of soup. Flavour with lemon juice, salt and pepper.

Because of its refreshing lemon flavour this soup is equally good served chilled. In summer, after liquidising this soup, I sometimes throw in a few fresh french beans broken into 1″ lengths, and cook gently until tender. As well as adding their own flavour they give a pleasant texture and colour contrast.

Leek and Carrot Soup

2 large carrots	nutmeg
4 leeks	salt and pepper
1 oz. butter	1 tbs. chopped parsley
1½ pints stock or water	

Prepare and dice carrots; wash and slice leeks, using as much green as possible. Sauté together in the butter for 10 minutes without browning. Add stock or water and cook gently for 30–40 minutes until vegetables are tender. Liquidise all but a good ladleful of soup, which is lcft as it is, to give texture and colour. Season with nutmeg, salt and pepper; add chopped parsley.

Leek and Potato Soup

This is a soup recipe with a bonus, because from the following ingredients not only can a delicious soup be made but also a leek vinaigrette salad as well.

2 pints water or stock	*for leek vinaigrette*
6 good-sized leeks	
2 large floury potatoes	3 tbs. sunflower seed oil
salt and pepper	1 tbs. white wine vinegar
1–2 oz. butter to serve	salt and pepper

Boil water. Meanwhile remove roots from leeks, slit down one side and clean carefully under running water. Cut off green parts and chop those that are worth keeping. Peel and dice potatoes. Throw whole leeks,

31

chopped green and potatoes into the boiling water and simmer for 15 minutes or so until leeks are very tender. Using perforated spoon, remove the six whole leeks and drain back into soup. These are the salad. Place them on a flat dish into which has been mixed 3 tbs. sunflower seed oil; 1 tbs. white wine vinegar, and salt and milled black pepper to taste. Baste leeks with the vinaigrette and leave until quite cold.

To finish soup pass through a medium coarse mouli or liquidise, season and serve with a good dab of butter in each bowl.

Obviously one would not serve both dishes at the same meal.

Minestra Soup

1 large potato	bouquet garni – 1 bayleaf,
1 large carrot	few parsley stalks,
2 sticks celery	sprig thyme
a few leaves cabbage,	8 oz. can baked beans
chopped	2 oz. macaroni
3 medium onions	salt and pepper
2 cloves garlic, crushed	chopped fresh basil
1 oz. butter	(when available)
15 oz. can tomatoes	grated cheese to serve
1½ pints stock or water	

Prepare vegetables and cut into dice. Sauté onion and garlic gently in the butter for 5 minutes, then add other vegetables and stir for a further 5 minutes. Add tomatoes, roughly chopped, stock or water and bouquet garni. Simmer for 20–30 minutes, until vegetables are just tender. Ten minutes before serving add baked beans and macaroni in 2″ lengths, and cook until macaroni is just tender. Season with salt and pepper, sprinkle with chopped fresh basil leaves when available, and serve very hot with grated cheese.

This hearty peasant soup makes an ideal 'complete'

meal accompanied by a simple tossed green salad, and followed by fresh fruit.

Cream of Mushroom Soup

$\frac{1}{2}$ lb. button mushrooms	$\frac{3}{4}$ pint milk
$\frac{3}{4}$ pint water	3 parsley stalks
1 oz. butter	salt and black pepper
2 tbs. flour	small carton single cream or top milk

Wash and slice mushrooms; simmer gently in the water for 5 minutes; drain, and reserve liquid. Melt butter in a clean pan and add flour; stir well until it bubbles, then remove from heat, and gradually beat in milk and mushroom liquid. Add parsley stalks and seasoning and simmer gently for 10 minutes. Remove stalks. Add mushrooms and heat through, then pour in cream. Check seasoning. Do not allow to boil again.

Thick Mushroom Soup

1$\frac{1}{2}$ lbs. potatoes	$\frac{1}{2}$ lb. button mushrooms or stalks
$\frac{1}{2}$ oz. butter	
1 bayleaf	1 heaped tbs. flour
1 pint water or stock	$\frac{1}{2}$ pint milk
	salt and pepper
	grated cheese to serve

Peel and cube potatoes; sauté lightly in the butter with the bayleaf for 5 minutes, but do not brown, then add water. Simmer gently until potatoes are tender, then add mushrooms or mushroom stalks, washed and sliced, and flour blended with the milk. Season with salt and pepper, and simmer for 10 minutes. Ladle into heated bowls and hand round plenty of grated cheese and tossed side salads for a quickly made complete meal. Finish with fresh fruit.

French Onion Soup

6 medium-sized onions
½ oz. butter
2 pints water or stock
bouquet garni – a bay-
    leaf, a sprig each of
    parsley and thyme
    tied together

1 tsp. marmite
1 heaped tbs. flour
salt, sugar and black
    pepper
grated cheese to serve

Slice onions and sauté in the butter until golden. Add water, bouquet garni and marmite, and simmer for 10–15 minutes until onions are tender. Add flour, blended with a little stock or water, simmer for a further 10 minutes to allow flour to cook. Taste, and season carefully with salt, a dash of sugar if necessary, and plenty of freshly ground black pepper. Serve as it is, or in traditional French manner, poured over toasted french bread in a piping hot bowl and topped with grated cheese, which can be made golden and bubbly under a hot grill. Accompanied by a green salad, this makes a perfect supper.

Parsnip Soup

½ lb. parsnips
1 carrot
1 potato
1 onion
1 bayleaf
1 oz. butter

¾ pint water
¾ pint milk
ground mace
salt and pepper
chopped fresh herbs or
    croûtons to garnish

Peel and chop parsnip, carrot, potato and onion. Sauté with bayleaf in the butter for 10 minutes without browning. Add the milk and water and cook for 45 minutes, remove bayleaf. Liquidise, and season with a little ground mace, salt and pepper. Serve garnished with chopped fresh herbs or croûtons.

Potato Soup

1 lb. potatoes	salt and pepper
1 onion	chopped chives or parsley for
3 cloves	garnish
1 bayleaf	1 small carton of single
1 oz. butter	cream or soured cream
2 pints water or stock	(optional)

Peel and roughly dice potatoes; peel onion and stick the cloves into it. Sauté potatoes, onion and bayleaf in the butter very gently for 10 minutes without browning and with the lid on the pan, then add the stock and simmer until potatoes are tender. Remove onion and bayleaf and liquidise or sieve soup. Season with salt and pepper; serve, as it is, good and hot and homely, or with a swirl of single cream or a dollop of soured cream and some chopped chives or parsley in each bowlful.

This soup can be made more nourishing by using half stock and half milk, or 2 parts stock to 1 part milk.

Spinach Soup

1 potato	1 $\frac{1}{2}$ pints water or stock
1 onion	nutmeg, salt and pepper
1 oz. butter	1 tsp. lemon juice
1 lb. spinach, or 1 large	$\frac{1}{4}$ pint evaporated milk or
pkt. frozen spinach	single cream

Peel and chop potato and onion and sauté lightly in the butter without browning for 5 minutes. Add well-washed and chopped spinach, or the block of frozen spinach and water. Simmer for 15–20 minutes until potatoes are tender. Liquidise, season carefully with nutmeg, salt and pepper, and lemon juice. Pour into heated bowls and pour a little cream into each bowl immediately before serving in a swirl of white against the dark green soup.

Cream of Watercress Soup

2 bunches watercress	salt and pepper
½ oz. butter	2 heaped tsp. flour
1 pint stock or water	½ pint milk

Wash watercress, only discarding really coarse stalks. Chop finely and sauté in the butter, tossing frequently over a gentle heat for 2–3 minutes. Add stock or water and seasoning, cover and simmer gently for 20–30 minutes. Add the flour, blended with the milk, bring to the boil, stirring, and cook very gently for 10 minutes. Check seasoning.

CHILLED SOUPS

Chilled Apple Soup

1 ½ lbs. cooking apples	sugar or clear honey to taste
1 ½ pints water	2 tsp. cornflour
pared rind ½ lemon	finely chopped apple mint
1″ cinnamon stick	and fresh or soured cream to serve

Peel, core and finely slice apples. Simmer gently in the water with the thinly pared lemon rind and cinnamon until tender. Remove cinnamon, and liquidise all but one good ladleful of apple slices, which remain to give texture to the soup. Sweeten to taste with sugar or honey, then pour in cornflour blended with a little cold water, and stir until thickened. Simmer for a further 5 minutes. Chill. Ladle into chilled bowls; add a whirl of cream – soured or fresh, according to taste, round and round into each bowl, and finish with a sprinkling of chopped apple mint for a very refreshing, cooling dish.

Variation: Chilled Plum Soup is made in exactly the same way, using 1 ½ lbs. ripe red plums (stoned) instead of apples.

Chilled Avocado Soup

$\frac{3}{4}$ pint water
thinly pared rind of
  $\frac{1}{2}$ lemon
1 bayleaf
small piece of onion
4 parsley stalks

1 avocado pear
juice $\frac{1}{2}$ lemon
$\frac{1}{4}$ pint single cream
salt and pepper
few chopped chives to serve

Put water, lemon rind, bayleaf, onion and parsley stalks into pan and simmer gently for 15 minutes. Strain. Peel and slice avocado and liquidise with the strained liquor and the lemon juice. Cool, then add cream and season to taste. Serve chilled and sprinkled with chopped chives.

Chilled Cucumber Soup

1 large cucumber
small carton sour cream
small carton natural
  yoghurt

salt and pepper
chopped chives or parsley

Peel cucumber; liquidise with the sour cream and yoghurt. Season to taste. Chill and serve sprinkled with chopped chives or parsley. Very easy and delicious on a lazy hot summer's day.

Gazpacho

2 medium-sized onions
1 clove garlic
1 large green pepper
6 tomatoes
2 tbs. oil

1 pint tomato juice
rind and juice 1 lemon
salt and pepper
$\frac{1}{2}$ cucumber

Peel and chop onions; crush garlic; dice pepper finely. Skin and slice tomatoes. Sauté onions, half the pepper and half the tomatoes in the oil for 10 minutes without browning. Add the tomato juice and lemon rind, removed thinly with a potato peeler. Simmer for a further 10–15 minutes. Liquidise. Add lemon juice and seasoning, and chill. Meanwhile, dice cucumber just before serving, and add to soup with other reserved vegetables. Hand round croûtons or crusty french bread to accompany.

Makes an unbeatable summer lunch or supper meal with the addition of plenty of grated gruyère cheese or marigold cheese, and followed by fresh fruit.

Garnishes for Soups

Basil, fresh and chopped – a perfect finish to a tomato-based soup, or minestra.

Celery leaves – chopped and added just before serving; especially good with celery, potato or carrot soup.

Cheese, grated – a little adds a pleasant savoury taste to a tomato or vegetable soup; more makes a good bowl of soup into a meal. For french finish put chunks of toasted french bread into hot bowls, fill up with soup and cover with cheese; put under moderately hot grill until golden and bubbly.

Chives, chopped – add a refreshing flavour and gorgeous colour to almost any soup. Particularly good with potato and beetroot soups.

Cream, fresh – single cream, poured round and round into bowls of soup, making white swirls, is a delightful garnish, especially to deep red beetroot soup or dark green spinach soup.

Cream, soured – may be thinned down with a little milk and used similarly; is particularly good with beetroot soup.

Croûtons – give a crunchy texture that enhances any soup, particularly a smooth liquidised soup. Make by shallow-frying $\frac{1}{4}''$ cubes of bread in a mixture of half butter and oil until evenly browned. Drain, cool and store in a tin.

Cucumber – thinly sliced, pretty with white soups, especially a chilled cucumber soup.

Egg – grated hard-boiled egg makes a pretty and nutritious garnish, particularly on white or pale coloured soups.

Lemon peel – slivers of lemon peel, pared off finely with a potato peeler, and snipped into $\frac{1}{2}''$ shreds, make a colourful, flavoursome and unusual garnish. Add to tomato, carrot or beetroot soup, also chilled fruit soups.

Lemon slices – slices of lemon, floated on the top of soup, are refreshing as well as pretty.

Marjoram – chopped fresh and used judiciously adds a very pleasant flavour to cabbage, cauliflower and vegetable soups.

Mint – chopped fresh mint is good with beetroot soup, potato soup and also chilled apple soup.

Mushroom slices – lightly fried, add colour and flavour to white soups.

Onion rings – sliced raw onion rings give crunchy texture, flavour and colour contrast to dark soups.

Onions, spring – as for onion rings – the green sprouts of winter onions can also be used for garnishing.

Orange peel – as for lemon peel, for an unusual flavour, and a very pretty colour.

Paprika – very good sprinkled fairly lavishly over white or pale soups.

Parsley, chopped – good with almost any soup.

Pepper rings – red and green, finely sliced, make a very pretty garnish, especially with sweetcorn soup.

Thyme, fresh chopped – piquant and good with a bland soup; use judiciously.

Tomato slices – add colour to pale soups.

III

SALADS AND STARTERS

So many ingredients can be used in salads: traditional salad items such as lettuce, cucumber, tomatoes, beetroot, radishes, spring onions and watercress combining with different fruits and vegetables such as carrots, cabbage (red and white), mushrooms, apricots, pears, peppers, melon, olives, cherries, strawberries, chicory, endive, apples, oranges, salsify, grapes, turnips, swedes, bananas, peaches, artichokes, fennel, asparagus, okra, lemon, avocado, grapefruit, aubergines, raisins, coconut, celery, dates, beans, sprouts, cauliflower, pineapple, ginger, fresh herbs to provide colour and variety throughout the year. Add varied and exciting dressings to these, some containing protein for the meal, as well as various nuts, cheeses (including cottage and cream cheese), eggs, yoghurt, sometimes served simply and sometimes made into dips, pâtés and moulds, and the possibilities are endless.

Since many salads, being essentially light, refreshing and palate-cleansing, make ideal starters or appetisers, and many pâtés, hors d'oeuvres and dips may equally well be served to provide protein in a salad meal, I have considered salads and starters together, and divided this chapter into five sections: in the first will be found recipes for vegetable and fruit salads of all types; in the second, dressings and dips; the third section contains recipes for pâtés, mousses and light savouries; the fourth for savouries on toast; and the fifth deals with garnishes and accompaniments which give crispness and texture to salads and starters where necessary – things such as melba toast, garlic bread and cheese shortbreads.

Recipes will serve four as main meals or six to eight as starters.

Vegetable and Fruit Salads

Antipasto Salad

½ lb. button mushrooms	2 heads chicory
2 tbs. vegetable oil	½ cucumber
1 small red pepper	6 tomatoes
2 tsp. wine or cider vinegar	4 hardboiled eggs
salt and pepper	½ lettuce
1 bunch radishes	12 olives
½ bunch spring onions	french dressing to serve

Wash and slice mushrooms; sauté lightly in 1 tbs. oil for 5 minutes – leave to cool. Slice red pepper very thinly, discarding seeds. Place on a flat dish and sprinkle with remaining oil and wine or cider vinegar. Toss well and season with salt and pepper. If possible, leave for 1-2 hours to soften. Meanwhile, wash and trim radishes and spring onions; slice chicory downwards into quarters, and cucumber, tomatoes and eggs into circles. Arrange all attractively on a bed of lettuce on a large platter or individual dishes, garnish with olives and serve with french dressing.

This is a typical gay Italian type salad, but its ingredients may be infinitely varied to suit taste and season. The more contrast in texture, flavour and colour, the better. Can be served with cubes of creamy cheese, instead of egg, for protein, perhaps first tossed in chopped chives or paprika.

Apple and Ginger Salad

4 dessert apples	2″ piece cucumber
1 piece preserved	1 tbs. syrup from ginger
stem ginger	to serve – lettuce,
1 orange	watercress or chicory

Peel and dice apples; finely chop ginger; remove peel and pith from orange and cut flesh into segments; dice cucumber. Mix all ingredients together and serve on a bed of watercress, lettuce or chicory.

Variation: 2 tbs. raisins plumped in a little boiling water for 10 minutes and then drained, or 2 tbs. chopped walnuts can also be added.

Small portions of this make very good starters. As a salad **meal** it is particularly good with cheese mousse, p. 74 or with cottage cheese dressing, p. 71.

Stuffed Apple Salad

4 dessert apples	few drops orange flower water
juice of ½ lemon	(optional)
2 oranges	1 lettuce
4 oz. black grapes	cottage cheese dressing,
1 banana	p. 71 to serve
1 tsp. clear honey	2 oz. toasted almonds

Slice apples in half across; scoop out flesh, being careful not to cut into apple skin. Brush lemon juice inside apple 'cups' thus formed. Chop the apple flesh removed, discarding core. Toss in lemon juice. Cut peel and pith from oranges; chop flesh, and mix with apple, grapes halved and stoned, and banana peeled and sliced. Toss well together, sweeten with clear honey, and add a few drops of orange flower water, if using.

Arrange apple 'cups' on a bed of crisp lettuce, pile fruit filling into the 'cups', top with a good whirl of cottage cheese dressing and shower with toasted almonds.

If using as a starter, half an apple per person is enough, and the mixture should not be made too sweet.

This makes a very pretty salad. In winter it is nice served on a base of cabbage and honey salad, p. 50, or chicory leaves.

Artichoke Salad

2 cans artichoke hearts	2 tomatoes
1 lettuce	1 oz. melted butter
$\frac{1}{2}$ bunch watercress	1 tbs. fresh chopped tarragon or chives

Drain artichoke hearts. Line a serving dish with lettuce; pile artichoke hearts in centre and surround with watercress and sliced tomatoes. At last minute pour melted butter over artichokes and sprinkle with tarragon or chives, and serve immediately, with a light protein dish such as stuffed eggs or on its own, in individual dishes, as a starter.

Asparagus and Cucumber Salad

$10\frac{1}{2}$ oz. can asparagus or 8 oz. pkt. frozen asparagus, cooked	2 tbs. natural yoghurt
	1 tsp. chopped fresh mint
1 cucumber	1 lettuce
salt	1 lemon
2 tbs. mayonnaise	little paprika

Drain and chop asparagus. Finely slice cucumber, sprinkle with salt and leave for 30 minutes, then drain off liquid and mix with asparagus, mayonnaise, natural yoghurt and mint. Serve on crisp lettuce leaves, garnished with lemon slices and a sprinkling of paprika. For an extra dash of colour, a garnish of red pepper could be added.

This makes a delicate and tempting starter, or, with

a protein dish such as stuffed eggs, p. 78, or cheese mousse, p. 74, or simply with a good cheese board and crusty bread it makes a light special luncheon or supper.

If there is some sour cream handy, use $1\frac{1}{2}$ tbs. of sour cream, 1 tbs. yoghurt and $1\frac{1}{2}$ tbs. mayonnaise for dressing.

Aubergine and Tomato Salad

2 large aubergines	salt and pepper
1 clove garlic, crushed	2 tsp. chopped fresh
6 tbs. yoghurt	chives or parsley
6 tomatoes	$\frac{1}{2}$ lettuce and $\frac{1}{2}$ lemon to serve

Wipe aubergines. Place on a dry baking sheet and bake at 350 °F., gas mark 4, for 30 minutes, until tender enough for a knife to be inserted easily. Cool. Chop and mix with the garlic, crushed to a paste in a little salt, yoghurt and tomatoes, skinned and sliced. Season with salt and pepper. Serve piled up on crisp lettuce, garnished with lemon slices and sprinkled with parsley.

Serve with melba toast, p. 84, or crispbreads or thin brown bread and butter if this is served as a starter. If using as a salad it goes well with a sweetcorn or asparagus quiche, p. 102.

For a simpler meal try it with crusty rolls or garlic bread, p. 84, and cheese.

Variation

Aubergine and Mushroom Salad

Make exactly as above, but with $\frac{1}{2}$ lb. button mushrooms instead of tomatoes. Wipe mushrooms and sauté gently in oil until tender.

Avocado and Grapefruit Salad

2 grapefruit	$\frac{1}{2}$ lettuce
2 oranges	1 tbs. chopped mint if
2 avocado pears	available

44

Using serrated knife cut peel and pith from grapefruit and oranges and slice out segments. Thinly peel, stone and slice avocados, and add to the grapefruit and oranges. Pile on to lettuce leaves and serve chilled and sprinkled with chopped mint if available, or halve grapefruit to remove flesh and serve mixture in the skins.

You may like to add a little sugar, but the salad should not be too sweet, rather refreshing.

A very good starter – but can also be served as a salad meal, perhaps with cottage cheese dressing, p. 71, hardboiled eggs or a cheese board to provide protein.

Avocado and Mushroom Salad

2 avocados	salt and pepper
$\frac{1}{2}$ lb. button mushrooms	$\frac{1}{2}$ lettuce
juice $\frac{1}{2}$ lemon	lemon slices and black
3 tbs. oil	olives to garnish

Thinly peel and slice avocados; wipe and slice mushrooms. Mix together with the lemon juice, oil, salt and pepper, and leave in a cool place for 1–2 hours, tossing from time to time. Serve on a base of lettuce, garnished with lemon slices and black olives. This is very good as a starter, served with thinly sliced buttered brown bread, but it also makes a delicious salad meal, and tartex pâté, p. 78, or stuffed eggs, p. 78, go especially well with it.

Variation
Avocado and Tomato Salad

Use 6 skinned, sliced tomatoes instead of mushrooms.

Stuffed Avocado with Egg and Chives

2 large avocados	drop or two of tabasco
juice 1 lemon	salt and pepper
4 hardboiled eggs	1 tbs. chopped chives
2 tbs. mayonnaise	lettuce or watercress to serve
1 tbs. tomato purée	

Halve and stone avocados and brush with half the lemon juice. Liquidise eggs with remaining lemon juice, mayonnaise and tomato purée. Add tabasco, salt and pepper to taste. Finally stir in the chopped chives. Pile into avocado halves. Serve chilled with lettuce or watercress.

Stuffed Avocado with Cottage Cheese

2 large avocados
juice $\frac{1}{2}$ lemon
8 oz. cottage cheese
1 clove garlic
1 oz. chopped walnuts

2 tomatoes
$\frac{1}{2}$ small green pepper
salt, pepper and paprika
lettuce and watercress
  to serve

Halve avocados, remove stones, brush cut surfaces with lemon juice. Sieve, liquidise or beat cottage cheese smooth; combine with crushed garlic, chopped walnuts, skinned and sliced tomatoes, very finely chopped green pepper. Season to taste. Pile into avocado halves; sprinkle with paprika. Serve on a bed of lettuce, garnished with watercress.

Stuffed Avocado Hors D'Oeuvre

2 large avocados
juice $\frac{1}{2}$ lemon
4 tomatoes
$\frac{1}{2}$ lb. button mushrooms

1 tbs. oil
1 oz. chopped walnuts
lemon slices, watercress
  and lettuce to serve

Prepare avocados as in previous recipes, brushing cut surfaces with lemon juice. Skin and slice tomatoes; wipe and finely chop mushrooms and fry lightly in the oil; when tender mix with the tomatoes and walnuts. Pile into avocado halves, garnish with lemon slices and serve on a bed of lettuce and watercress.

Serve as an hors d'oeuvre. Can also be used as a main meal, but some protein will need to be added to the meal – perhaps some brie cheese and crusty bread, or can be topped with a good whirl of cottage cheese dressing, p. 71.

Banana and Carrot Salad with Coconut Cream Dressing

2 oz. raisins	bunch watercress
2 large carrots	4 oranges
4 large bananas	coconut cream dressing, p. 71
juice $\frac{1}{2}$ lemon	toasted coconut strands to garnish

Wash raisins and leave for 10 minutes in hot water to plump. Peel carrots and grate coarsely. Skin and slice bananas and toss in the lemon juice with the carrots and raisins. Place in the centre of a large serving dish or individual plates, and surround with watercress and orange slices. Serve with coconut cream dressing poured over, and a garnish of toasted coconut strands if available – otherwise use a few chopped nuts or a little finely grated orange rind.

Can also be piled on to a base of crisp lettuce or chicory leaves.

With its protein rich dressing this makes a complete meal served with crunchy digestive biscuits.

Beetroot Salad

$\frac{1}{2}$–$\frac{3}{4}$ lb. raw beetroot	1 lettuce
4 apples	1 bunch watercress
4 sticks celery	lemon slices to garnish
4 tbs. raisins	cottage cheese dressing,
6 tbs. oil	p. 71, or sour cream
2 tbs. red wine vinegar	dressing, p. 73
or cider vinegar	1 tbs. chopped chives
peel of $\frac{1}{2}$ lemon	

Peel and coarsely grate raw beetroot and apple, add finely sliced celery, raisins, oil and vinegar. Remove peel from lemon using a potato peeler, then snip into $\frac{1}{2}''$ slivers using scissors; add to mixture. Allow to marinade for an hour or so if possible. Serve on bed of lettuce, bordered by lemon slices and topped with cottage cheese dressing, or sour cream dressing. Finish with a sprinkling of chopped chives. The suggested dressings also provide protein for this meal.

Beetroot and Onion Salad

8 cooked beetroots	2 oz. chopped walnuts
honey dressing, p. 72	1 bunch watercress
1 lettuce	salt and pepper
1 onion	

Skin and slice beetroots; toss in honey dressing. Pile beetroot in the centre of serving dish lined with lettuce leaves. Slice onion and arrange over beetroot; sprinkle with chopped walnuts. Surround with watercress. Serve with cottage cheese dressing, p. 71, or sour cream dressing, p. 73, or hardboiled eggs, or crispy almond slices, p. 82, for protein.

Variation

Beetroot and Yoghurt Salad

Omit onion, and top with 1 carton of natural yoghurt.

Broadbean and Yoghurt Salad

1 lb. broadbeans in pod	small carton natural
lemon dressing	yoghurt
salt, pepper and sugar	lemon slices to garnish
1 lettuce	1 tbs. chopped chives

Wash beans and if tender enough, top and tail and slice in their pods into $\frac{1}{2}''$ lengths, otherwise remove beans from pods; cook in a little boiling water until tender. Drain and toss hot beans in lemon dressing; allow to get quite cold, basting from time to time. Serve piled up on lettuce, topped with natural yoghurt, with a garnish of lemon slices and a sprinkling of chopped chives. Very good with cheese mousse, p. 74, or roasted cashewnut pâté, p. 78.

Brussels Sprout Mayonnaise

1 lb. brussels sprouts
4 carrots, grated
2 tbs. lemon juice
4 tbs. mayonnaise
4 tbs. chopped dates
1 bunch watercress
snipped slivers of lemon and
    orange rind to garnish

Wash and coarsely grate sprouts; peel and finely grate carrots. Mix together with lemon juice, mayonnaise and dates. Serve with watercress, and garnish with the lemon and orange rind.

As a starter or side salad very small portions are needed, with perhaps a base of crisp lettuce heart. As a main meal, serve with a protein savoury. It is very good with a sprinkling of toasted flaked almonds, or salted cashewnuts to add crispness, and goes well with roasted cashewnut pâté, p. 78, tartex pâté, p. 78, a slice of celery chaudfroid, p. 80, or one of the quiches in the next chapter.

Gay Cabbage Salad

1 lb. cabbage
2 large carrots
1 red pepper
1 celery heart
garlic french dressing, p. 72
4 tomatoes
lettuce leaves and
    watercress to serve

Shred the cabbage finely, grate the carrot fairly coarsely, de-seed and shred the pepper, wash and chop celery and mix all ingredients together in the dressing. Leave for an hour or more to marinade. Just before serving add the tomatoes, skinned and sliced. Check seasoning, and serve on a bed of lettuce leaves, garnished with watercress. Very good with a creamy savoury, such as cheese mousse, p. 74, egg and mushroom pâté, p. 77, or, simply, with grated cheese and for a more substantial winter meal, jacket baked potatoes.

Cabbage and Honey Salad

1 lb. white cabbage   honey dressing, p. 72

Shred cabbage finely. Mix with honey dressing, and if possible leave for at least one hour before serving.

This is cabbage salad at its simplest. The blend of honey and cabbage is surprisingly good. Many things can be added to vary this basic salad: chopped tomato, raisins, flaked roasted almonds or pinekernels, chopped green or red pepper, celery, pineapple, apple, banana, grated carrot, dates, etc. Or it can be topped with sour cream dressing, p. 73, and garnished with orange slices and toasted almonds for a specially delicious meal.

Cabbage and Apple Salad

1 lb. cabbage	2 oz. sultanas
4 rosy apples	honey dressing
	chicory or lettuce for serving

Wash and finely shred cabbage; wipe apples and chop without peeling. Plump sultanas in boiling water for 10 minutes; drain, and mix with cabbage. Toss ingredients thoroughly in dressing. Serve on a bed of chicory or lettuce, with a protein savoury, grated cheese or hardboiled eggs.

Variations

Red Cabbage and Apple Salad

Make as above, but use 1 lb. red cabbage. Garnish with chopped walnuts.

Cauliflower and Apple Salad

Make as above, but use 1 lb. cauliflower (1 medium cauliflower) instead of cabbage.

Cabbage and Pineapple Salad

Is delicious; use 1 lb. shredded white cabbage; mix with the drained contents of a 15 oz. can of pineapple pieces (or, if fresh pineapple is available, use this – delectable!) and moisten with french dressing, p. 72, or honey dressing, p. 72.

Carrot and Almond Salad

1 lb. carrots
1 small apple
½ green pepper (optional)
¼ pint natural yoghurt
   or mayonnaise

1 lettuce
2 oz. toasted almonds
1 tomato, fresh parsley
   and 1 lemon for
   decoration

Scrape and finely grate carrots and apple; chop pepper if using. Add enough mayonnaise or natural yoghurt – or a mixture – to moisten. Serve on a bed of crisp lettuce and top with a generous scattering of toasted almonds. Garnish with tomato and lemon slices and sprigs of fresh parsley.

Cauliflower Salad

1 small cauliflower
¼ pint mayonnaise or
   natural yoghurt
1 tbs. lemon juice
2 oz. sultanas

½ lettuce
4 tomatoes
1 tbs. chopped mint
1–2 tbs. toasted nuts

Wash and coarsely grate cauliflower. Mix with the mayonnaise or yoghurt, lemon juice and sultanas. If using yoghurt, mixture may need sweetening with a little honey. Pile in centre of lettuce leaves arranged on a large plate or individual dishes. Garnish with tomato slices, sprinkle with mint and scatter with toasted nuts.

Like the previous recipes, Cauliflower Salad goes well with a crisp textured savoury.

Cheese and Tomato Salad

8 large tomatoes
honey dressing, p. 72
1 head chicory or half
  lettuce
8 oz. grated cheese

1 tbs. chopped parsley,
  chives or mint
1 tsp. chopped onion
1 bunch watercress

Skin tomatoes only if necessary – slice and toss in a little honey dressing. Arrange on a base of chicory or lettuce leaves. Finely grate cheese and mix with chopped herbs and onion, and sprinkle over tomatoes. Garnish with watercress.

Chicory Salad

4 heads chicory
4 large carrots
2 oz. sultanas
$\frac{1}{4}$ pint mayonnaise, p. 73,
  or natural yoghurt

a few lettuce leaves to
  serve
1 oz. toasted almonds

Cut chicory into rings; finely grate carrots. Plump sultanas in boiling water for 10 minutes, then drain and add to chicory and carrot, and mix with mayonnaise or yoghurt. Serve on lettuce leaves, garnished with toasted almonds.

If serving as a starter do not make too rich – less mayonnaise may be needed, sharpened with a little lemon juice, or use the yoghurt version.

As a salad, this goes well with a crisp textured rather simple savoury.

Chicory, Orange and Grape Salad

4 large oranges
4 oz. black grapes
2 oz. chopped walnuts
honey dressing, p. 72

salt and pepper
4 heads chicory
6 oz. gruyère or gouda
  cheese

Cut peel from oranges and slice into segments; mix with halved and pitted grapes and walnuts. Toss in honey dressing, and serve on a base of chicory leaves with slices of gruyère cheese.

Chicory and Tomato Salad

8 tomatoes	salt and pepper
4 heads chicory	$\frac{1}{2}$ tsp. brown sugar
french dressing	1 bunch watercress or mustard and cress

Skin and quarter tomatoes. Wash and slice chicory. Toss together in french dressing and season with salt, pepper and sugar as necessary. Serve with watercress or cress.

A few black olives are very good tossed in with this salad. It goes well with cheese dishes – cheese mousse, p. 74, for instance, or a savoury cheese quiche, or simply bread and a good cheese board, or baked potatoes and grated cheese.

Stuffed Chicory Salad

4 heads chicory	2 oz. chopped brazilnuts
4 oz. raisins or sultanas	1 bunch watercress
large carton (8 oz.) cottage cheese	2 oranges

Cut chicory in half lengthwise; remove heart from each half, leaving a 'boat'. Finely chop hearts. Plump raisins or sultanas by plunging in boiling water for 10 minutes; drain. Chop, and mix with cottage cheese, chopped brazilnuts and chopped chicory centres. Pile chicory boats with this mixture; serve on a bed of watercress, surrounded by rings of peeled and pithed oranges.

Cucumber and Tomato Salad

1 cucumber
6 tomatoes
2 tbs. chopped chives
  or onion green
salt and pepper
6 tbs. oil

2 tbs. wine vinegar
sugar
½ lettuce
½ lb. soft, creamy cheese –
  see recipe

Wipe and dice or coarsely grate cucumber; wash and slice tomatoes, and mix all together with chopped chives. Season with salt and pepper. Mix together oil and vinegar, add a touch of sugar, and pour over cucumber mixture; toss well. Line serving dish with lettuce; pile cucumber mixture into centre and surround with slices of a creamy textured but sliceable cheese, such as demisel, camembert or brie. A gorgeous salad for summer months when one can afford to be generous with cucumbers and tomatoes.

Cucumber and Yoghurt Salad

1 large cucumber
salt and pepper
¼ pint natural yoghurt

pinch dill (optional)
1 tbs. chopped parsley
  or mint
crisp lettuce leaves

Slice cucumber finely, with skin if tender. Sprinkle with salt and leave for 30 minutes, then drain off and discard liquid. Mix with the yoghurt, herbs and salt and pepper to taste. Serve on crisp lettuce leaves.

An excellent starter served with melba toast, p. 84, but equally good as a salad meal when accompanied by a protein savoury.

Dried Fruit Salad with Cottage Cheese Dressing

4 oz. dried apricots	1 lettuce
4 oz. prunes	cottage cheese p. 71 or sour
4 oz. sultanas	cream dressing, p. 73
4 oranges	1 oz. toasted almonds
½ head celery	

Cover apricots, prunes and sultanas with boiling water and leave to soak overnight. Cut skins from oranges and slice fruit into pieces. Slice celery; mix altogether. Arrange on a bed of lettuce with dressing poured over, and garnish with toasted almonds.

A useful salad for winter.

Endive Salad

1 head curly endive	4 tomatoes
1 tbs. lemon juice	2 oz. roasted cashewnuts
6 tbs. mayonnaise or	
natural yoghurt	

Wash endive, discarding any discoloured or damaged leaves. Chop fairly finely and toss in the lemon juice. Mix with the mayonnaise or yoghurt, perhaps adding a touch of sugar to taste, and arrange in the centre of serving dish. Slice tomatoes into thin rings and arrange round endive. Roughly chop the nuts and sprinkle over the tomatoes. Serve with an additional protein savoury, such as stuffed eggs, p. 78.

Fennel Vinaigrette

2 large fennel bulbs	1 tbs. chopped parsley
juice of 1 lemon	½ lettuce
salt and pepper	4 tomatoes
3 tbs. oil	lemon slices

Wash, trim and finely slice fennel. Mix with lemon juice, salt, pepper and oil. Sprinkle with chopped parsley and serve surrounded by lettuce leaves and garnished with tomato and lemon slices. Very good with cheese mousse, p. 74, egg moulds, p. 76 or egg and mushroom pâté, p. 77.

Fruit and Cheese Salad

$\frac{1}{2}$ lb. creamy but firm
    cheese
$\frac{1}{4}$ lb. white grapes
$\frac{1}{4}$ lb. black grapes
1 orange
2 apples

2 pears
1 banana
juice of $\frac{1}{2}$ lemon
2 heads chicory or $\frac{1}{2}$ head
    lettuce

Cube cheese; halve and de-seed grapes; remove rind and pith from orange and cut into segments; cube apples and pears and slice banana. Toss fruits in lemon juice to keep colour, then mix with cheese and serve on chicory or lettuce leaves.

Mixed Fruit Salad with Cottage Cheese Dressing

3 apples
2 pears
2 oranges
8 oz. black grapes or
    strawberries
2 peaches or 4 apricots
    if available

juice of 1 orange
crisp lettuce leaves
cottage cheese dressing,
    p. 71
2 oz. toasted flaked
    almonds

Wash fruits and slice into even-sized pieces; mix well and toss in orange juice; heap up on a bed of lettuce; pour cottage cheese dressing over the mixture and sprinkle with toasted almonds.

This is one of my favourite salads; its exact composition can be varied through the year according to what is available. Protein is contained in the dressing and garnish, making this salad a complete meal, slimming and full of vitality.

French Bean Salad

1 lb. french beans	1 lettuce
¼ pint mayonnaise or natural yoghurt or french dressing	salt and pepper
	1 lemon
	2 oz. toasted almonds
1 tbs. chopped parsley	

Cook beans until tender; drain and toss immediately in mayonnaise, natural yoghurt or french dressing. Leave to cool, then mix in parsley and lettuce, roughly torn, just before serving. Garnish with lemon slices and a good scattering of almonds. Serve this salad with a simple savoury.

Grapefruit Baskets

4 grapefruit	a little kirsch (optional)
½ lb. black grapes or cherries	3 tbs. flaked almonds (optional)

Using a sharp knife make two cuts in the grapefruit about $\frac{1}{8}''$ each side of the 'stalk', going half-way down the fruit. Insert the point of the knife at the base of one of these cuts and slice round, across the grapefruit until you get to the other cut. Remove knife, re-insert the other side and repeat process. These two sections of grapefruit should then fall away, leaving a basket shape, from which you cut away the fruit from the section under the 'handle'. Remove grapefruit flesh from the 'bowl' of the basket in the usual way with a grapefruit knife. Repeat the whole process with the other three grapefruit, then cut away all the pith and skin from the chunks of grapefruit thus produced. Mix the flesh with the stoned grapes or cherries, the kirsch and the nuts if liked. Pile mixture back into the baskets and serve on a bed of fresh green bayleaves, or other non-poisonous leaves available.

Variation: Canned drained mandarin oranges could replace the cherries.

Simple Green Salad

1 large lettuce
french dressing or
  garlic dressing

1 tbs. chopped fresh herbs,
  as available

Wash lettuce, dry and tear into pieces. When ready to serve toss in the dressing and sprinkle with fresh herbs to taste.

Leek, Apple and Tomato Salad

6 large dessert apples
4–6 tomatoes
2 small leeks

juice of $\frac{1}{2}$ lemon
salt and freshly ground
  black pepper
lettuce leaves to serve

Dice the apples, with the peel on if it is sound and attractive; cut tomatoes into small pieces and mix with the apple. Slit leeks and wash thoroughly, saving as much of the green part as possible, then slice very finely and mix with the apple and tomato, lemon juice, salt and pepper. Serve piled up on crisp lettuce leaves. This is a vegetarian favourite, and a very popular salad. It is useful during the winter, and even more delicious when topped with a good whirl of sour cream dressing, p. 73.

Leeks Vinaigrette

This salad belongs here. The directions are given with Leek and Potato Soup, p. 31, because, surprisingly, the two can be made at the same time – for serving at different meals.

Serve the leeks with watercress and tomatoes, and a savoury such as crispy almond slices, p. 82, or a quiche.

Stuffed Lettuce

2 firm hearty lettuces	1 small grated onion
½ lb. finely grated cheese	2 tomatoes
small carton cottage or cream cheese	chopped fresh herbs as available
2 tbs. mayonnaise or cream	honey and mint dressing, p. 72

Remove outer leaves from lettuce until firm, compact heart is reached; wash these outer leaves thoroughly, then slice top off lettuce heart and scoop out centre. Blend well together cheeses, mayonnaise or cream, grated onion and chopped centre of lettuce; pack lettuce cavities with this. Chill for 1–2 hours, then using sharp knife, cut lettuces into slices and serve on a plate which can be lined with the outer leaves of lettuce. Decorate with the tomatoes, sliced, and sprinkle with chopped fresh herbs as available. Serve with honey and mint dressing, p. 72.

Lettuce Wedge Salad with Cottage Cheese and Chive Dressing

2 firm hearty lettuces	cottage cheese and chive dressing, p. 71, or natural yoghurt and chives
a clove of garlic	
salt and pepper	
juice ½ lemon	lemon slices to garnish

Wash lettuces thoroughly without removing leaves and then cut into wedges. Crush garlic with the salt and mix with the lemon juice. Toss lettuce in this, then place on a serving dish. Top with cottage cheese and chive dressing, p. 71, or natural yoghurt blended with chives and garnish with lemon slices.

A very simple salad for when lettuces are cheap and plentiful. Dressing contains protein so this makes a complete, refreshing meal for a hot day.

Melon with Ginger

1 melon
2 pieces preserved
  stem ginger

4 tbs. liquid from ginger
lemon to garnish

Cut the melon in half; remove seeds, chop the flesh or make into balls, using a vegetable scoop. Chop the ginger finely and mix with the melon, adding the liquid from the ginger. Sweeten to taste if necessary – not too much – and serve in individual glasses, garnished with lemon, if liked.

Melon Wedge Salad

1 melon
lettuce or green salading
  to serve
8 oz. cottage cheese

2 tbs. cream
4 oz. black grapes or
  strawberries, sliced

Halve and then slice melon, remove seeds. Arrange slices on base of green salading. Liquidise cottage cheese and cream and mix with grapes or strawberries. Spoon mixture over melon slices.

Mushroom and Yoghurt Salad

1 lb. button mushrooms
2 tbs. vegetable oil
$\frac{1}{4}$ pint natural yoghurt
1 clove garlic

salt and pepper
1 lettuce
1 tbs. chopped chives or
  spring onion green

Wash mushrooms – do not peel. Slice and cook gently in the vegetable oil until tender. Cool, then mix with natural yoghurt, crushed garlic and salt and pepper. Serve piled up on lettuce base, sprinkled with chopped chives or spring onion green.

Nuttolene Salad

2 oz. sultanas

french dressing, p. 72

1 onion

2 green peppers

1 small can nuttolene

2 apples

½ lb. shredded white cabbage
moistened with honey
dressing p. 72 or ½ lettuce
or bunch watercress

Plump sultanas by leaving for 10–15 minutes in the dressing and then add onion and peppers, finely chopped, and coarsely grated nuttolene and apples. Serve piled up on a plate, with a surround of lettuce, or watercress, or shredded cabbage moistened with honey dressing.

Okra Salad

1 heart celery

4 tomatoes

½ cucumber

14 oz. can okra

garlic french dressing, p. 72

1 bunch watercress

Slice celery, tomatoes and cucumber; drain okra. Toss all together in garlic french dressing, and serve with watercress.

Orange, Apple and Celery Salad

4 oranges

4 apples

1 head celery

½ lettuce

cress to garnish

2 oz. walnuts

Cut peel and pith from oranges and slice into segments. Chop apples and celery. Mix all together and serve on lettuce with a garnish of cress and chopped walnuts.

Goes well with a soft-textured dish such as one of the egg pâtés, egg mousse or cream cheese and pineapple, p. 75.

Orange and Cucumber Salad

1 hearty lettuce	4 sprigs mint
4 large juicy oranges	sour cream dressing, p. 73,
1 cucumber	or natural yoghurt

Wash lettuce, reserving the crisp, inner leaves and shredding the others. Remove skin and pith from oranges and cut into segments. Coarsely grate cucumber; chop mint. Mix together with shredded lettuce, and arrange on serving dish, surrounded by the reserved, inner lettuce leaves. Serve with sour cream dressing or natural yoghurt.

Orange, Prune and Watercress Salad

4 oranges	1 head celery
2 bunches watercress	8 oz. prunes, soaked
(if unavailable use	overnight
1 lettuce or 2–3 heads	2 oz. chopped walnuts
chicory)	honey dressing, p. 72

Cut peel and pith from oranges, slice into thin rounds. Wash watercress, lettuce or chicory. Wash and slice celery, mix with prunes and nuts, and toss all together in honey dressing. Pile up on serving dishes, surround with watercress, lettuce or chicory and orange slices.

Stuffed Peach Salad

4 ripe peaches	4 oz. black grapes, sliced and
juice of $\frac{1}{2}$ lemon	stoned
8 oz. cottage cheese	2 oz. chopped walnuts
	lettuce leaves

Halve peaches and remove stones. Brush cut surfaces with lemon juice to prevent discolouration. Liquidise or sieve cheese, and mix with black grapes and walnuts. Spoon into peach halves and serve on lettuce leaves.

Can also be served as a light refreshing dessert – omitting lettuce leaves, of course!

Stuffed Pears

2 large pears
lemon juice
1 large piece preserved
  ginger in syrup

4 oz. carton cottage
  cheese or cream cheese
2 tbs. grated carrot
2 oz. chopped walnuts

Cut pears in half lengthwise; using teaspoon and sharp knife remove core and any stringy bits. Brush cut surfaces with lemon juice. Crush or chop ginger; combine with cheese, grated carrot and walnuts. Pile into pears.

Stuffed Pineapple Slices

1 ripe pineapple
4 oz. cream cheese
1 tbs. roasted cashewnuts,
  peanuts or toasted
  almonds

1 tbs. chopped ripe
  cherries or cocktail
  cherries
lettuce leaves

Using sharp knife cut leafy top and skin, from pineapple. Cut pineapple in half and using a grapefruit knife cut out hard core from each half to leave a neat hole. Combine cream cheese, nuts and cherries, and pack into pineapple. If possible chill for at least two hours, then slice. Line plate with lettuce leaves and arrange pineapple slices thereon.

Potato Salad Mould

1½ lbs. new potatoes
4 tbs. mayonnaise
1 clove garlic
few lettuce leaves
½ cucumber

½ cup peas, cooked
chopped mint
½ red pepper
4 tomatoes
½ bunch spring onions,
  chopped

Cook new potatoes in skins till tender. Rub off skins, dice potatoes and while still hot toss in mayonnaise – a little crushed garlic can be added, or a cut clove of garlic rubbed round mixing bowl. Pack firmly into oiled 1½ pint ring mould. Leave to cool, then turn out on to a plate lined with lettuce leaves. Dice cucumber and mix with peas and a little chopped fresh mint, pile into centre of ring. Cut pepper into strips and arrange over sides of potato ring. Cut circles of tomato and place round outside of ring and sprinkle with chopped spring onions.

This salad is good served with a hot cheese soufflé, p. 88, for a very satisfying meal.

Rice and Avocado Salad

8 oz. natural long grain rice	1 tsp. sugar
1 clove garlic	2 large avocado pears
3 tbs. oil	juice of 1 lemon
1 tbs. wine vinegar or cider vinegar	1 lb. tomatoes
salt and pepper	1 tbs. chopped parsley
	slices of hardboiled egg to decorate

Cook rice in plenty of boiling water, drain. While still hot mix with the crushed clove of garlic, oil and wine vinegar. Add salt, pepper and sugar. Cool, stirring from time to time. Meanwhile peel and stone avocados and slice flesh; toss in lemon juice; skin and slice tomatoes. Mix all lightly with rice and serve sprinkled with chopped parsley. This salad is good with simple green salad and decorated with hardboiled egg slices.

Summer Rice Salad

8 oz. natural long grain rice	2 tomatoes
1 tsp. turmeric powder	1 medium onion
8 oz. pkt. mixed frozen vegetables	$6\frac{1}{2}$ oz. red peppers
6 tbs. salad oil	4 oz. toasted almonds
juice 1 small lemon	pinch basil
$\frac{1}{2}$ tsp. paprika	salt and pepper
2 tbs. chopped parsley	4–6 hardboiled eggs
	lettuce, watercress, or parsley to serve

Cook the rice with the turmeric in plenty of fast-boiling water until just tender. Cook the frozen vegetables for about 5 minutes, drain. Meanwhile mix the oil, lemon juice, paprika and chopped parsley in a large bowl. Skin and finely chop the tomatoes and onion, drain and chop the peppers, and add all to the oil mixture, together with the nuts and basil. Drain the rice and frozen vegetables and add these to the mixture too. Mix well, season with salt and pepper, then press into a well-oiled 2-pint mould, and leave in a cool place for an hour or so. When ready to serve invert mould over a plate of lettuce (the shape should slide out easily and cleanly). Surround with sliced hardboiled eggs and sprigs of watercress or parsley.

Rice and Vegetable Salad

1 clove garlic	$\frac{1}{2}$-8 oz. can tomatoes
$\frac{1}{4}$ lb. onions	8 oz. long grain natural rice
2 tbs. sunflower oil	salt and pepper
$\frac{1}{2}$ lb. aubergine	2 drops tabasco
$6\frac{1}{2}$ oz. can red peppers	6 small flat mushrooms

Crush garlic finely; peel and chop onions. Fry in the oil for 15 minutes; do not brown. Chop aubergine and add to mixture; cook for a further 5–10 minutes until tender. Add canned peppers and tomatoes with liquid and cook for 10 more minutes. Cook rice in plenty of fast-boiling water until just tender. Drain thoroughly and run under cold tap. Mix with vegetables, season and add tabasco. Fry mushrooms lightly in oil. Line a 7" soufflé dish with foil, brush with oil, and place mushrooms in it, black side down, arranged attractively, then place rice mixture over them. Press down and leave in fridge over-night. Next day turn out and serve with green salad and cheese or egg for protein.

For a Special Presentation Rice Salad:

A 1½ pint ring mould can be used for any of the above rice mixtures. Press the mixture into a well-oiled mould. Turn out on to lettuce base and fill centre with sliced hardboiled egg tossed in cream, or mayonnaise, or cubes of creamy cheese, or roasted nuts.

Mixed Root Salad

2 parsnips	juice of 1 orange
1 turnip	1 tbs. sultanas
2 carrots	3 tbs. natural yoghurt
1 swede	salt and pepper
1 raw beetroot	1 small onion
3 tbs. mayonnaise	½ lettuce or 2 heads chicory
3 tbs. french dressing	mustard and cress
1 tsp. parsley	tomato slices

Peel and grate root vegetables into separate bowls. Mix the parsnips with mayonnaise, the turnip with french dressing and parsley, the carrots with orange juice and sultanas, and the swede with yoghurt, salt and pepper. Slice the onion into thin rings. Arrange the lettuce or chicory on serving plates, spoon on piles of the root vegetables, garnish with slices of tomatoes and cress. A very useful salad for winter.

Ratatouille Salad

Ratatouille, p. 144, is very good chilled and served with crisp green salading, grated cheese and crusty bread or croûtons.

Russian Salad Platter

½ lb. cooked new potatoes	2 cooked beetroots
½ lb. cooked carrots	2 tomatoes
½ lb. french beans	½ lemon
¼ pint mayonnaise	1 onion
salt and pepper	parsley
1 lettuce	

Mix together diced cooked potatoes, carrots, french beans and mayonnaise; season well. Pile up on base of lettuce; surround with thin slices of cooked beetroot, tomatoes, lemon and onion. Garnish with parsley. For a less rich version, mayonnaise can be replaced by natural yoghurt, or a mixture of the two.

Salata

1 clove garlic	3 tbs. olive oil
1 medium-sized mild onion	1 bayleaf
1 large green pepper	1 tbs. wine vinegar
2 medium carrots	salt and pepper
4 tomatoes	2 bunches watercress

Crush garlic; peel and slice onion; slice green pepper; scrape and coarsely grate carrots, slice tomatoes. Lightly fry in oil with a bayleaf for 5 minutes, then add wine vinegar. Chill and leave for at least 1 hour. Remove bayleaf and serve with watercress.

Salsify Mayonnaise

1 lb. salsify	1 tbs. parsley
1 tbs. lemon juice	1 bunch watercress
4 tbs. mayonnaise	4 tomatoes

Peel and cook salsify until tender. Toss while still hot in the lemon juice and mayonnaise. Cool. Pile in the centre of serving dish and sprinkle with parsley. Surround with watercress and tomato slices.

Spring Green Salad

1 clove garlic	2 tbs. cream
1 lb. good hearty spring greens	salt and pepper
	few roasted cashewnuts
4 tender new carrots	4 tomatoes
1 tbs. lemon juice	

Peel clove of garlic, slice in half and wipe round salad bowl. Finely shred cabbage, grate carrots, and mix all together with lemon juice, cream, salt and pepper. Serve with a garnish of roasted cashewnuts and sliced tomatoes.

Summer Salad Bowl

1 large crisp hearty lettuce	½ punnet mustard and cress sprig mint and parsley
4–6 fresh firm tomatoes	1 avocado pear (optional)
½ cucumber	juice of ½ lemon
small bunch radishes	salt and pepper
8 spring onions	french dressing, p. 72

Wash lettuce and either pull apart, or if firmly packed cut into eighths; wipe and slice tomatoes and cucumber; wash and trim radishes, onions and cress; chop herbs and mix all together. Add avocado, skinned, sliced and tossed in lemon juice. Just before serving pour french dressing over the mixture and toss well.

Sweetcorn Salad

11½ oz. can sweetcorn	½ lb. green cabbage
½ green pepper	honey dressing, p. 72
juice of ½ lemon	2 tomatoes

Drain sweetcorn, finely chop pepper and mix together with the lemon juice. Finely shred cabbage and moisten well with honey dressing. Arrange sweetcorn salad in a border of cabbage, and garnish with tomato slices.

Tomato Salad

1½ lbs. tomatoes	1 mild onion
french dressing, p. 72	a little fresh chopped basil or parsley
salt, pepper and sugar	few black olives to garnish (optional)

Skin tomatoes only if necessary, then slice and toss in french dressing, seasoning well with salt, pepper and sugar. Garnish with sliced onion, fresh chopped basil or parsley and black olives if using.

Serve as a starter on individual plates with a base of lettuce; or with crusty bread and cheese as a main course.

For when tomatoes are cheap and good!

Tomato Stuffed with Creamy Cheese

4 large tomatoes
salt and pepper
8 oz. cottage or cream cheese or demi-sel
1 tsp. chopped fresh basil

1 tbs. chopped onion
dash tabasco
green salad leaves to serve

Halve tomatoes, scoop out flesh. Sprinkle with salt; turn upside down to drain. Chop scooped-out tomato, mix with cheese, basil, onion, and a drop or two of tabasco, and salt and pepper. Pile back into tomato halves. Serve chilled on a bed of green salad.

Tomatoes Stuffed with Avocado

4 large tomatoes
egg and avocado pâté, p. 77, or avocado cream, p. 74

lettuce or chicory and watercress to serve

Prepare tomatoes as above. Reserve scooped-out tomato for use in another recipe – a soup or savoury – and fill tomatoes with the egg and avocado pâté or avocado cream. Serve on lettuce or chicory, garnished with watercress.

Tomatoes Stuffed with Mushrooms

4 large tomatoes	squeeze lemon juice
8 oz. mushrooms	parsley to garnish
1 tbs. oil	green leaves to serve
salt and pepper	

Prepare tomatoes as in previous recipe. Wash, chop and lightly fry mushrooms in oil. Cool and drain off excess liquid; add chopped tomato centres; season with salt, pepper and a little lemon juice. Pile into tomato 'cups'. Garnish with parsley and serve on green leaves.

If using as a main salad add protein – perhaps in the form of a dressing – sour cream dressing, p. 73, or cottage cheese dressing, p. 71, for instance.

Waldorf Salad

1 head celery	4 tbs. mayonnaise or natural
4 apples	yoghurt
2 oz. walnuts	lettuce leaves to serve

Thoroughly wash and then chop tender part of celery; core and dice apples, chop walnuts. Mix all together with mayonnaise or yoghurt. Serve piled up on lettuce leaves.

Alternatively, instead of the mayonnaise or yoghurt, this salad is very good served with cottage cheese dressing, p. 71, or sour cream dressing, p. 73, which also supply the protein for the meal.

SALAD DRESSINGS AND DIPS

Vegan Cottage Cheese

2 pints plant-milk   salt and pepper
4 tbs. lemon juice

Heat the plant-milk and lemon juice together in a pan until the plant-milk curdles and separates. Strain through muslin. Season curds to taste and use as required.

Coconut Cream Dressing

1 oz. desiccated coconut $\frac{1}{4}$ pint single cream or
8 oz. carton cottage cheese   top milk
                                $\frac{1}{2}$ tsp. honey

Liquidise all ingredients together. Serve with fruit salads. Can be served as a dip with crisp celery, apple, pear and pineapple pieces, and grapes.

Cottage Cheese Dressing

8 oz. carton cottage $\frac{1}{4}$ pint single cream or
    cheese   top milk

Liquidise together the cottage cheese and single cream or top milk. Serve poured over almost any salad to provide not only a delicious, not-too-fattening creamy dressing, but also plentiful protein.

Variations

Cottage Cheese and Chive Dressing

Make as above, adding 1–2 tbs. of finely chopped chives or spring onion green.

Cottage Cheese and Cucumber Dressing

Add $\frac{1}{4}$ cucumber and 2 sprigs of mint to above, and liquidise.

French Dressing

2 tbs. wine vinegar or lemon juice	salt and pepper
6 tbs. olive oil or vegetable oil or a mixture of both	1 desstsp. caster sugar

Whisk or liquidise ingredients together, or shake vigorously in jam jar. A little dry mustard can be blended with ingredients.

Variations

Garlic French Dressing
Is made by adding 1 crushed clove garlic to above.

Paprika Dressing
Add ½ tsp. paprika to above.

Parsley French Dressing
Add 1 tbs. chopped parsley to above.

Honey Dressing

1 tbs. clear honey	¼ tsp. salt
1 tbs. cider vinegar	black pepper
3 tbs. oil	

Thoroughly combine all ingredients.

Variation

Honey and Mint Dressing
Made by adding 1 tbs. chopped fresh mint or 1 tsp. concentrated mint sauce to above.

Lemon Dressing

1 lemon	salt and pepper
½ tsp. french mustard	1 desstsp. sugar
	6 tbs. oil

Peel lemon thinly using potato peeler; snip peel into thin shreds; squeeze juice. Whisk or liquidise together lemon juice, mustard, sugar, salt, pepper and oil. Add shredded peel.

Mayonnaise (Quick Method)

1 whole egg	$\frac{1}{2}$ pint oil – olive oil, or half
1 tsp. salt	olive, half vegetable oil
$\frac{1}{2}$ tsp. brown sugar	2 tbs. wine vinegar or lemon
1 tsp. french mustard	juice

The egg must be at room temperature. Break into liquidiser. Beat thoroughly with the salt, sugar and mustard. Add oil a little at a time until mixture begins to thicken, then add more quickly to make a smooth, thick mayonnaise. Finally mix in vinegar or lemon juice. Will keep in a cool place for at least a week.

Mayonnaise and Yoghurt Dressing

Blend together equal quantities of mayonnaise and yoghurt for a not-too-rich dressing which will add a little extra protein to the salad too.

Sour Cream Dressing

8 oz. carton cottage cheese	salt and pepper
$\frac{1}{4}$ pint sour cream	

Liquidise together the cottage cheese and sour cream. Season with salt and pepper for a delicious protein-rich dressing.

Soya Mayonnaise

2 tbs. soya flour	salt and pepper
$\frac{1}{2}$ tsp. french mustard	2 tbs. cider vinegar or
1 tsp. sugar	lemon juice
	4 tbs. oil

Mix together the soya flour, mustard, sugar, salt, pepper and cider vinegar or lemon juice to make a smooth cream. Gradually add the oil, a little at a time so that the mixture doesn't curdle, and beat until thick.

If it does curdle, a vigorous beating with a whisk will put it right. A useful recipe for vegans.

Pâtés, Mousses and Light Savouries
Avocado Cream

2 avocado pears
juice ½ small lemon
6 oz. cottage cheese
1 tbs. mayonnaise or
cream

2 tbs. finely chopped chives or
½ tsp. finely grated onion
salt and pepper
paprika, lemon twist and
parsley to garnish

Peel and stone avocado pears, toss in lemon juice;
liquidise with cottage cheese, mayonnaise or cream, and
chives or onion; or chop avocado finely and mix all
ingredients together. Season carefully with salt and
pepper. Spoon into pottery crock and smooth with fork,
or heap up on a serving dish. Sprinkle with a little
paprika, and garnish with a lemon twist and parsley.

Cheese Mousse

4 tbs. liquid – milk
or dry white wine
2 oz. grated gruyère
cheese
2 oz. grated parmesan
cheese

3 eggs, separated
½ pint evaporated milk or
single cream
1 clove garlic
3 tsp. agar agar
tiny pinch mustard

Heat 4 tbs. liquid in pan, remove from heat, add
cheese and stir until melted. Beat in egg yolks. Bring
evaporated milk or cream to the boil with clove of garlic;
when boiling sprinkle on agar agar. Cook for 1 minute,
remove garlic, and pour milk over cheese mixture, add
mustard, and lastly fold in egg whites. Turn into wetted
1-pint mould to set.

This may be presented more elaborately for special
occasions:

Use 1 pint mould and when set turn out. Liquidise
4 oz. cottage cheese with 1 tbs. single cream. Use this to
pipe on top of mould, round base and down sides, using

shell nozzle. Decorate with black and white grapes, and toasted flaked almonds.

Chutney in the Raw

1 lb. stoneless dates	1 pint vinegar
1 lb. sultanas	1 tsp. salt
1 lb. apples	pepper
1 lb. onions	dash cayenne, allspice and
1 lb. brown sugar	ground ginger

Mince first four ingredients together and stir in sugar and vinegar. Add 1 tsp. salt, sprinkling of pepper, dash of cayenne, a little allspice and ground ginger. Stand for 24 hours, giving the mixture a stir from time to time, then bottle – makes 6–7 lbs. This is a quick-to-make chutney and keeps well.

Cream Cheese and Pineapple

½ fresh pineapple	2 tbs. whipped cream
8 oz. cream cheese	(optional)

Remove skin and hard centre from pineapple, dice and mix into cream cheese, lastly adding whipped cream, if using. Cream cheese rather than cottage cheese has to be used for this dish, as the latter, when combined with fresh pineapple, has a bitter taste. If canned pineapple is used instead, cottage cheese can be used, however. The resulting creamy savoury can be served in three different ways. (1) Heaped up on a dish and garnished with more pineapple or a simple salad. (2) Pressed into a simple mould – a jelly mould, or ring mould – chilled and turned out. A ring mould is particularly suitable and the centre looks attractive with grapes or strawberries when in season. (3) If the pineapple is cut carefully right down the centre and the fruit scooped out, the cream cheese mixture can be piled into the resulting pineapple 'shell' to make the centre of an attractive salad platter.

Variation

Cream Cheese with Date and Nut

This is made exactly as above, except that cottage cheese could be used instead of cream cheese – useful for weight-watchers! Mix the cheese until creamy – I like to sieve cottage cheese for extra smoothness, then add 4 oz. chopped dates and 2 oz. chopped nuts.

Egg and Tartex Pâté Cocktail

1 tbs. mayonnaise	1 small can tartex
1 tsp. tomato purée	(vegetable pâté)
1 tsp. lemon juice	1 hardboiled egg
1 tbs. single cream	¼ cucumber
pinch paprika	1 lettuce heart
1 drop tabasco	1 tomato
salt and pepper	1 lemon, sliced

Blend together mayonnaise, tomato purée, lemon juice and cream; season with paprika, tabasco, salt and pepper; slice tartex and hardboiled egg; dice cucumber. Mix with mayonnaise dressing. Shred lettuce heart – use to line individual dishes; spoon on egg and tartex mixture; garnish with tomato and lemon slices.

Egg Moulds

4 hardboiled eggs	¼ tsp. mace
½ tsp. marmite	salt and pepper
1½ tsp. agar agar	½ tbs. parsley
½ pint water	watercress, lettuce and
¼ pint evaporated milk	tomato to garnish
or single cream	

Shell eggs and chop finely. Dissolve marmite in the water and when it is boiling, sprinkle agar agar over and whisk until dissolved; boil gently for 1–2 minutes. Remove from heat, add eggs, evaporated milk or single

cream, mace and salt and pepper. Pour into wetted
1-pint mould to set. Turn out, sprinkle with chopped
parsley, and surround with a little watercress or lettuce
and sliced tomato.

Egg and Avocado Pâté

4 eggs, hardboiled	1 avocado pear
2 tbs. mayonnaise	1 tbs. chopped parsley
2 tbs. whipped cream	few drops tabasco
2 tbs. lemon juice	lemon slices, fresh parsley and
1 clove garlic	lettuce leaves to serve
salt and pepper	

Liquidise the hardboiled eggs with mayonnaise,
cream and 1 tbs. of the lemon juice. Wipe cut clove of
garlic round mixing bowl and mix egg in this. Cut
avocado in half, peel as thinly as possible and remove
stone. Cut into small slices and toss in the remaining
lemon juice, then add to the egg mixture; season to
taste and add parsley and a drop or two of tabasco.
Spoon into a pottery crock and chill, or heap on to
lettuce leaves and garnish with lemon twists. Serve with
melba toast, p. 84.

Variations

Egg and Mushroom Pâté

Omit avocado; use 6oz. sliced and sautéed mushrooms.

Egg and Pepper Pâté

Use 1 finely chopped large green pepper instead of the
avocado.

Egg and Asparagus Pâté

Use 1 can of asparagus spears drained and chopped
instead of avocado. May be liquidised with 2 tbs. asparagus liquid and 2 tbs. cream.

Egg and Tartex Pâté

Omit avocado; use 1 large can tartex and 2 oz. toasted
almonds or pinekernels; mix well with the eggs.

Stuffed Eggs

6 hardboiled eggs	1 tsp. tomato purée
1 large can tartex (vegetable pâté)	1 tbs. mayonnaise
	salt and pepper
2 drops tabasco	chopped parsley or chives
1 tsp. lemon juice	a little lemon to garnish

Halve eggs lengthwise and remove yolks. Mash well with tartex, tabasco, lemon juice, tomato purée and mayonnaise. Using large shell nozzle pipe into the egg whites. Garnish with chopped parsley or chives, and a small piece of sliced lemon.

Tartex and Almond Pâté

1 large can tartex	$\frac{1}{2}$ tsp. paprika
4 oz. ground almonds	3 oz. flaked almonds – preferably toasted
1 clove garlic, crushed	
1 tsp. tomato purée	salt and pepper
1 tsp. lemon juice	lemon, and a few lettuce leaves to garnish
2 tsp. finely chopped parsley	

Mash together tartex, ground almonds, garlic, tomato purée, lemon juice, parsley, paprika and 2 oz. of the flaked almonds. Season with salt and pepper. Make into a round or square shape on a plate, coat sides with the rest of the flaked almonds, smooth top with a fork, chill, and firm. Garnish with lemon, surround with lettuce and serve in slices with brown bread and butter.

Roasted Cashewnut Pâté

1 clove garlic	dash of tabasco
8 oz. cream cheese	1 tsp. fresh garden herbs as available
4 tbs. top milk or single cream	
4 oz. roasted cashewnuts	pepper

Crush garlic and beat with cream cheese and top of milk or cream until smooth. Mill half of the nuts and chop the rest. Stir into the cheese mixture with tabasco, fresh herbs, and a grating of pepper. Press into a pottery crock and chill. Serve with melba toast, p. 84, or brown bread and butter, or as a savoury with a salad.

Asparagus Chaudfroid

1 can green asparagus spears	8 oz. ground almonds
1 small onion	8 oz. soft white breadcrumbs
2 oz. butter	2 eggs
1 bayleaf	2 heaped tbs. chopped parsley
6 peppercorns	grated nutmeg
1 tbs. flour	salt and pepper
approx. $\frac{1}{4}$ pint milk – see recipe	lettuce leaves and lemon slices to garnish

Drain asparagus, reserving liquid. Chop all but 4 best spears of asparagus; leave on one side. Peel and grate onion; cook gently in the butter with the bayleaf and peppercorns until tender but not browned. Remove bayleaf and peppercorns, add flour, then gradually pour in asparagus liquid made up to $\frac{1}{2}$ pint with milk, stirring until thickened. Remove from heat and add almonds, breadcrumbs, beaten eggs and chopped parsley. Season with nutmeg, salt and pepper, then lightly fold in chopped asparagus, being careful not to mash it. Line a 2 lb. bread tin with foil and brush with oil. Arrange best asparagus spears in bottom, then gently spoon in mixture. Cover with foil and steam for 2 hours. Allow timbale to cool before carefully turning out of tin. Decorate with crisp lettuce leaves and lemon slices. This timbale can be glazed for special occasions. To do this, boil $\frac{1}{2}$ pint water with 1 bayleaf, 4 peppercorns, a piece of onion and some parsley sprigs; let the mixture stand for 15 minutes, then strain mixture and bring it to the boil again; sprinkle with 1 level tsp. of agar agar, whisking until dissolved. Mixture can then be brushed or spooned over the top of the timbale and left to set. Agar agar, a vegetable gelatine, can be obtained from health food stores.

Variations

Celery Chaudfroid

Replace asparagus with head of celery, very finely chopped. Garnish with red pepper or tomato slices and parsley.

Fennel Chaudfroid

Use $\frac{1}{2}$ lb. fennel, finely chopped, instead of the asparagus and sauté with the onions.

Pimento Chaudfroid

Chop, and fry with the onions, a clove of garlic and a $6\frac{1}{2}$ oz. can of peppers, finely chopped. Season with a few drops of tabasco. Make liquid from pimentos up to $\frac{1}{2}$ pint with milk. Serve with sour cream dressing, p. 73.

SAVOURIES ON TOAST

Asparagus and Cheese on Toast

1 small can asparagus   4 pieces hot buttered toast
8 oz. grated cheese

Drain asparagus – keep liquid for soups but put 1 tbs. into a pan and add the cheese. Melt over gentle heat, then add asparagus and heap on to hot toast slices. Grill until golden brown and bubbly. Serve at once with a tossed green salad

Avocado, Tomato and Almonds on Toast

juice of $\frac{1}{2}$ lemon   4 pieces hot buttered toast
2 avocado pears   8 oz. curd, cottage or
2 tomatoes   cream cheese
salt and pepper   2 tbs. flaked almonds
                     lemon slices

80

Put lemon juice into a bowl; remove skin and stone from avocados and slice into bowl; skin and slice tomatoes, add to avocados, season with salt and pepper. Spread the toast with the cheese, put the avocados and tomatoes on top and sprinkle with almonds. Place under moderate grill just to heat through. Serve garnished with lemon slices.

Mushroom and Cheese on Toast

8 oz. button mushrooms	8 oz. grated cheese
1 oz. butter	4 pieces hot buttered toast

Wash and slice mushrooms, fry lightly in the butter until tender, then add the cheese and melt over a gentle heat. Heap on toast and grill until golden brown.

Pineapple and Cheese on Toast

small can pineapple pieces	4 pieces hot buttered
8 oz. grated cheese	toast

Make as for Asparagus and Cheese on Toast, above.

Tomato and Cheese on Toast

6 tomatoes, skinned	8 oz. grated cheese
1 oz. butter	4 pieces hot buttered toast

Make as for Mushroom and Cheese on Toast, above.

Tomato, Nuts and Onion on Toast

8 tomatoes, skinned	juice of $\frac{1}{2}$ lemon
1 oz. butter	salt and pepper
4 oz. very finely grated nuts	4 pieces hot buttered toast
	lemon slices or onion slices
1 tsp. grated onion	to garnish

Chop tomatoes and cook gently in the butter for

3 minutes. Add nuts, onion, lemon juice, salt and pepper. Cook for a further few minutes to heat through thoroughly, then heap on toast and garnish with lemon or onion slices.

Tartex Pâté and Tomatoes on Toast

6 tomatoes
1 oz. butter
1 large can tartex vegetable pâté

4 tbs. finely milled nuts
juice of $\frac{1}{2}$ lemon
4 pieces hot buttered toast

Skin and chop tomatoes, cook gently in the butter for 3 minutes, then beat in the tartex, nuts and lemon juice, also a little milk, if necessary, to moisten. Cook for a further few minutes to heat thoroughly. Spread on toast and serve at once.

Tartex Pâté and Mushrooms on Toast

$\frac{1}{2}$ lb. mushrooms
1 oz. butter
1 large can tartex vegetable pâté

4 tbs. finely milled nuts
juice of $\frac{1}{2}$ lemon
4 pieces hot buttered toast

Make as for Tartex Pâté and Tomatoes on Toast, above.

ACCOMPANIMENTS FOR SALADS AND STARTERS

Crispy Almond Slices

4 oz. weetabix
4 oz. ground almonds or other nuts, grated finely
4 oz. margarine

4 oz. flaked almonds or chopped nuts
1 clove garlic, crushed
$\frac{1}{2}$ tsp. mixed herbs
salt and pepper

Crumble weetabix, mix with ground almonds or other ground nuts, and rub in margarine as for pastry, until fine crumb stage is reached. Add flaked almonds, crushed garlic, mixed herbs and seasoning. Press into buttered swiss roll tin, and bake at 450 °F., gas mark 8, for 15–17 minutes, until golden brown and crisp. Cut into triangles and serve hot or cold with creamy salads or hot vegetable mixtures to add protein and crisp texture to the meal.

Toasted Almonds

Flaked almonds are best for this. They can be spread on a baking sheet and placed in a moderate oven for about 10 minutes until golden and crisp. Or a small quantity can be placed in a dry saucepan and stirred over a moderate heat until all are evenly browned. Pine-kernels can be treated in either way.

Cheese Shortbread

8 oz. plain wholemeal flour	8 oz. grated cheese – cheddar or half cheddar, half parmesan
salt and pepper	
dash of cayenne	6 oz. butter or margarine

Sift flour with salt, pepper and cayenne; mix with cheese; rub in butter to make a dough which will hold together. Check seasoning. Roll into a sausage shape and slice evenly. Place slices on a baking sheet and bake at 375 °F., gas mark 5, for 20–30 minutes, until golden brown. Cool on tins. Store in airtight tins. Another way of adding crispness and protein to a soft-textured meal. The same mixture can be rolled out and cut into long thin slices to make cheese straws.

Croûtons

Cut stale bread into $\frac{1}{2}''$ cubes. Deep fry until golden and crisp. Drain on absorbent kitchen paper. These keep well stored in an airtight tin. Can be made smaller if required.

Croûtes

Cut stale slices of bread into triangles, rounds – or any shape you like. Fry on both sides in hot oil; drain on kitchen paper, and serve where crispness is needed.

Garlic Bread

2 cloves garlic   4 oz. butter
salt   small french loaf

Crush garlic in a little salt and blend into butter. Make deep slices in loaf but do not cut right through. Carefully spread both sides of each slice with the garlic butter; wrap in foil; place on baking tray and bake 10–15 minutes at 450 °F., gas mark 8. Serve hot.

Melba Toast

Lightly toast slices of bread on both sides. While still hot cut through each slice using a sharp serrated knife. Place on grill rack or in moderate oven to toast the newly-cut side. Toast will curl up attractively.

Salted Nuts

Heat a little vegetable oil in frying pan. Toss blanched almonds, cashewnuts, or pinekernels in this, turning frequently until all are evenly golden. Drain on absorbent kitchen paper; dust with salt, or salt and a touch of cayenne. When quite cold store in airtight tin. These brown more evenly if only a few are fried at a time.

IV

VEGETARIAN MAIN COURSE SAVOURIES

The recipes in this chapter are for hot, cooked main meals. They use the vegetarian forms of protein which sound so boring when listed as eggs, cheese, nuts, pulses and textured vegetable proteins, but which form the basis of many delectable dishes. In many cases these can be presented simply, or, with imaginative garnishing, more elaborately for special occasions – many people do not realise how really colourful and mouthwatering such dishes can be.

A few of the ingredients – for instance, toasted almonds – are expensive, but contain very little waste, if any. Also, not having the expense of meat, perhaps we may be allowed to be a bit extravagant now and again with interesting and unusual vegetables and garnishes!

CHEESE SAVOURIES

In the following recipes – and indeed throughout this book – the cheese used, unless otherwise stated, is cheddar, preferably the Marigold vegetarian cheddar. Recipes using cheese as a subsidiary ingredient are classified under the other sections in this chapter – the rice, pasta and vegetable sections. It's always a help, if one can remember, to grate up plenty of cheese at a time, and store it in a polythene container in the fridge, for future, perhaps more hectic, occasions.

Fondue

16 oz. gruyère or gouda
  cheese
1 level tbs. cornflour
2 tbs. kirsch

½ pint dry white wine
1 clove garlic
salt, pepper and nutmeg
1 french loaf to serve

Grate cheese. Blend cornflour to a smooth paste with 2 tbs. of the wine and the kirsch. Cut clove of garlic and wipe round heavy-bottomed pan; add cheese and white wine to pan; cook over gentle heat until cheese melts, then pour in the cornflour mixture and stir until thickened. Simmer for 4–5 minutes. Season with salt, pepper and nutmeg.

Place piping hot pan of fondue in centre of table, preferably over a candle-burner; serve with a basket of warmed french bread cubes for everyone to take it in turns to spear with their fork and turn in the delicious fondue. The brown, sticky crust at the bottom of the pan is the best part of all.

A super, quick late night dinner for a few friends. I like to serve a mixed green salad with this meal.

For a more economical version, use gouda cheese, and cider instead of the white wine, and forget the kirsch! Not at all 'classical' – but still very good.

Fondue is also good as a rich sauce with delicious vegetables such as globe artichokes, courgettes or as the sauce accompanying Vegetable Platter, p. 141.

Gnocchi

1 pint milk
1 bayleaf
4 oz. semolina
4 oz. grated cheese

½ tsp. dry mustard
grated nutmeg, salt and pepper
½ oz. butter

Heat milk with bayleaf; when boiling sprinkle on the semolina, stirring until thick. Cook gently for 3–4 minutes, then remove from heat and add 2 oz. of the grated cheese, $\frac{1}{2}$ tsp. dry mustard, nutmeg, salt and pepper. Turn mixture on to a large flat wetted plate, and spread to a depth of about $\frac{1}{2}''$. Leave until quite cold, then cut into rounds using a wetted $1\frac{1}{2}''$ cutter. Place rounds in rows, overlapping like roof tiles. Sprinkle with rest of grated cheese, and dot with the butter. Place under a moderately hot grill for 15–20 minutes until crisp and golden. Serve with tomato sauce, and a green vegetable.

Fried Gnocchi

Make mixture as above; cut gnocchi into rounds or squares, dip in beaten egg and crumbs. Deep or shallow fry until golden and crispy. Serve with lemon slices and parsley sauce, lemon sauce or sauce piquante.

Roulade au Parmesan

4 eggs, separated	*filling:*
a few drops tabasco or some cayenne	small can chopped asparagus
3 tbs. parmesan cheese, grated	a little butter
	$\frac{1}{2}$ tsp. flour
2 tbs. soft breadcrumbs	small carton double cream
salt and pepper	1 tsp. chopped parsley
	1 tbs. lemon juice

Beat yolks to make them smooth, then add tabasco or cayenne and fold in egg whites, cheese, breadcrumbs and seasoning. Turn into a swiss roll tin which has been lined with foil and well brushed with oil or melted butter. Bake in a hot oven, 425 °F., gas mark 7, for 8–10 minutes until the mixture springs back when touched lightly. Turn out on to a piece of greaseproof paper, peel off foil, spread with filling, and using the greaseproof underneath to help, roll up and slide on to a warm serving dish. Decorate with parsley, and serve immediately.

Filling

Drain asparagus and toss in the butter over a gentle heat, then add flour and cream and heat until thickened; stir in parsley and lemon juice and season to taste.

EGG SAVOURIES

As with cheese dishes these are not always easy to classify, but I have included in this section recipes which use eggs as the main ingredient. More recipes using eggs appear in other sections of the book combined with such ingredients as rice, pasta and vegetables and classified under those headings.

The eggs used in this section are standard free range (see p. 2) unless otherwise stated.

Banana Eggs

2 medium onions	1 tbs. chopped parsley
1 clove garlic	2 tomatoes, skinned and
$\frac{1}{2}$ oz. butter	sliced
6 bananas, skinned and	$\frac{1}{2}$ tsp. turmeric
chopped	salt and pepper
1 green pepper, chopped	6 eggs

Sauté the sliced onions and the garlic, crushed, in the butter until brown, then add the rest of the ingredients, except for the eggs, and cook all together until soft. Put into a largish shallow ovenproof dish and make six hollows. Break eggs into the hollows and bake in a moderate oven, 350 °F., gas mark 4, for about 15 minutes until eggs are set.

Cheese Soufflé

3 oz. butter	4 eggs, separated
2 heaped tbs. flour	$\frac{1}{2}$ tsp. dry mustard
$\frac{1}{2}$ pint milk	salt and pepper
6 heaped tbs. grated cheese	

Melt butter, add flour; when mixture froths remove from heat and stir in milk. Return to heat, stirring until mixture thickens. Remove from heat and add grated cheese; allow to cool slightly, then mix in egg yolks, mustard and a seasoning of salt and pepper. Whisk whites until very stiff and fold into mixture. Turn into a greased 2-pint soufflé dish, and bake in a fairly hot oven at 400 °F., gas mark 6, for about 40 minutes until well-risen and golden brown. Serve immediately with a tomato sauce, mushroom sauce or wine sauce.

Variations

Spinach Soufflé

Add 1 large packet frozen chopped spinach purée instead of cheese. Cook spinach according to directions on packet; drain and add to soufflé with egg yolks. Serve with tomato sauce.

Tartex Soufflé

Omit cheese and use 1 large can tartex, 2 tbs. tomato purée, 1 tsp. grated lemon rind, 1 tbs. lemon juice. Serve with wine sauce, lemon sauce, green herb sauce, onion sauce or mushroom sauce.

Asparagus Soufflé

Make as above, omitting cheese and using a 10 oz. can of asparagus; make liquid up to $\frac{1}{2}$ pint with milk and use instead of the milk in recipe. Add chopped asparagus to the sauce with the egg yolks. Serve with lemon sauce.

Mushroom Soufflé

Use $\frac{1}{2}$ lb. button mushrooms. Chop and fry lightly in the butter before adding the flour. Cheese can be used or omitted as desired. Serve with tomato sauce.

Egg Croquettes

4 hardboiled eggs
good knob of butter
4 oz. bread
½ tsp. marmite

1 tbs. chopped parsley
salt and pepper
2 raw eggs
crumbs for coating
oil for frying

Chop the eggs very finely and mix with butter. Make bread into crumbs; add to eggs with marmite, chopped parsley, salt and pepper, and 1 of the raw eggs to make a stiff paste. Mould into balls, dip in egg and bread crumbs and fry in hot oil. Drain and serve garnished with parsley sprigs. Tomato sauce, or sauce aurore goes well with this dish.

Egg Curry

6 eggs
1 large onion
8 tbs. vegetable oil
2 tsp. white mustard seed
2 tsp. ground coriander
2 tsp. ground cumin seed
2 tsp. turmeric

2 tbs. flour
1 pint water
4 tbs. tomato purée
½ oz. coconut cream*
salt and pepper
cooked rice to serve

Hardboil the eggs, shell and slice and keep warm and covered in the ovenproof serving dish you will be using for the curry. Peel and chop onion and fry gently in the oil until tender, then add the spices and cook for a further minute or two until the mustard seeds start to 'pop'. Stir in the flour, add the water and tomato purée and simmer gently for 10 minutes, then add the coconut cream, salt and pepper. Pour over the hardboiled eggs. Serve with cooked rice.

*Coconut cream can be bought from health shops and keeps for ages in the fridge. If you haven't any to hand, however, use instead 4 tbs. desiccated coconut and pour over 1 pint boiling water. Leave for 10 minutes and strain well, pressing out all the liquid which can be used in the recipe instead of water.

Egg Fu Yong

2 large onions	1 tbs. soy sauce
1 can bean sprouts	salt and pepper
4 eggs	

Chop onions finely; drain bean sprouts. Beat eggs well. Mix all ingredients together, seasoning well with salt and pepper. Fry in hot deep fat, a ladleful at a time. Drain well and serve with boiled rice or crispy egg noodles.

To make crispy noodles, cook 4–6 oz. egg noodles in fast boiling water until tender. Drain, rinse and pat dry on a clean teacloth. Fry in deep oil until crisp and golden. Drain well.

Oeufs Florentine

4 eggs	½ pint cheese sauce, p. 153
1 lb. spinach	2 oz. grated cheese
salt and pepper	1 oz. crumbs for topping
½ oz. butter	

Poach eggs in boiling water until just cooked. Meanwhile wash spinach and cook in a pan without any water; drain very well and add the salt, pepper and almost half of the butter. Butter a shallow casserole; spread a layer of spinach in the bottom, on to this put the eggs and cover with the cheese sauce. Sprinkle with the grated cheese and crumbs, and dot with the rest of the butter. Brown under a moderately hot grill. Oeufs florentine are also very good made in individual ramekins.

Pipérade

1 large clove garlic	2 oz. butter
4 large onions	salt and pepper
6 tomatoes, peeled	4–6 eggs, beaten
2 large red or green peppers	croûtons, toast, rolls or fried bread to serve
½ tsp. marjoram	

Crush garlic; slice onions and tomatoes; de-seed and chop peppers and sauté with the marjoram in the butter over a gentle heat with the lid on the pan for 20–30 minutes until mixture is very soft – almost purée-like, in fact. Season with salt and pepper. Pour in eggs and stir gently until lightly set. Check seasoning. Serve with croûtons, toast, rolls or fried bread.

Pipérade can be served for a good quick supper, perhaps accompanied by a simple green side-salad, with fresh fruit to finish the meal.

Quick Soufflé Omelette

6 eggs, separated	salt and pepper
1 oz. flour	2 oz. grated cheese
	knob of butter

Preheat the grill to a good brisk heat while preparing the mixture. Separate eggs and whisk whites until stiff; leave on one side while beating yolks with flour until smooth and creamy, then fold in egg whites, seasoning and grated cheese. If possible, use a pyrosil casserole to melt butter in – otherwise use a frying pan. Pour egg mixture into the piping hot butter and fry quickly until underneath is cooked; then place under the hot grill to cook the top and finish the soufflé. Serve immediately with a tossed green salad for a very quick meal.

Stuffed Eggs with Savoury Sauce

6 eggs, hardboiled	*for sauce :*
$\frac{1}{2}$ oz. butter	$\frac{3}{4}$ pint sauce béchamel, p. 152
1 tbs. grated onion	$\frac{1}{4}$ pint mayonnaise
$\frac{1}{2}$–1 tsp. curry powder	juice 1 lemon
1 tbs. tomato ketchup	$\frac{1}{4}$ tsp. paprika
salt and pepper	chopped parsley and lemon
$\frac{1}{2}$ tsp. lemon juice	slices to serve

Slice hardboiled eggs in half lengthwise. Carefully

remove yolks. Leave whites on one side. Mash yolks finely. Melt butter and lightly fry onion and curry powder to taste, then mix in all the other ingredients (except egg whites) and blend to a smooth paste. Spoon into egg whites, arrange in a casserole and keep warm. Make a good sauce béchamel and add mayonnaise, lemon juice, paprika and maybe a little curry powder; pour most of sauce over eggs and make all piping hot in oven or over moderate flame. Garnish with a little chopped parsley and lemon slices. Serve rest of sauce separately. Serve with boiled rice.

Variation

Stuffed Eggs Mornay

Stuff eggs exactly as above, but cover with $\frac{3}{4}$ pint cheese sauce, p. 153, top with 1–2 oz. breadcrumbs and grated cheese, and brown under a moderate grill.

Tomato Baked Eggs

4 large tomatoes	salt and pepper
4 eggs	$\frac{1}{2}$ pint cheese sauce, p. 153

Remove top of tomatoes and scoop out pulp – this will not be needed but can be used up in salads, soups or sauces. Place tomato 'cups' in a buttered casserole and break an egg into each. Top with cheese sauce and bake eggs in a moderate oven, 350 °F., gas mark 4, for 20 minutes until set. Serve immediately, with a tossed green salad or cooked spinach.

FRITTERS AND PANCAKES

Crispy and light, fritters and pancakes are always popular, and are especially good when combined with vegetables and sauces. Fritters need to be served as soon as possible after cooking, but pancakes can be made well ahead, cooled on a wire rack and kept stacked in a plastic box in the fridge (or well wrapped in the deep freeze) until required. A supply of these ready-made pancakes makes good quick meals. Roll the pancakes round a vegetable filling (which can be anything from chopped tomato to asparagus and cream), place snugly in a buttered casserole, cover with cheese sauce, and make golden and bubbly in the oven. Canned aubergines, okra, creamed sweetcorn and creamed mushrooms make handy quick fillings for pancakes, and protein in the form of cheese or flaked or grated nuts can be added to the filling or included in the topping sauce.

Savoury Stuffed Pancakes

pancakes
4 oz. wholemeal flour
$\frac{1}{2}$ tsp. salt
1 egg
$\frac{1}{2}$ pint water

savoury filling
3 tomatoes, skinned
2 oz. wholemeal bread

1 onion
1 clove garlic
1 oz. butter
3 oz. walnuts
$\frac{1}{2}$ tsp. mixed herbs
1 tbs. tomato purée
$\frac{1}{2}$ tsp. yeast extract
salt and freshly ground
    black pepper
$\frac{3}{4}$ pint cheese sauce, p. 153

Chop tomatoes and mash with the bread, crusts removed. Leave on one side to soften bread Chop onion, crush garlic and sauté in the butter until tender. Meanwhile mill the nuts, using a fine electric or rotary hand grater or liquidiser, and add to the onions with the breadcrumbs and tomato mixture, mixed herbs, tomato purée and yeast extract. Season well with salt and pepper. (Or use pineapple stuffing, p. 127.)

Make pancake mixture by sifting together flour and salt, making a well and adding egg and water; beat well until smooth. Allow to stand for $\frac{1}{2}$ an hour if possible. Fry pancakes on one side only in a very little fat and pile up on a plate; keep warm – or make well in advance, cool and store in a plastic box in the fridge or deep freeze. Spread cooked side of pancakes with filling, roll up and place cosily side by side in warmed ovenproof dish. Pour cheese sauce over the pancakes and bake at 350 °F., gas mark 4, for 20 minutes.

Variations

Stuffed Pancakes with Asparagus Filling

Drain and chop the contents of 1 can of asparagus and mix with a good tablespoonful of mayonnaise, a tablespoonful of whipped cream, salt, pepper and a squeeze of lemon juice.

Stuffed Pancakes with Aubergine Filling

Sauté a medium-sized aubergine in a little oil, with a bayleaf, 4 tomatoes, a crushed clove of garlic and an onion, chopped. When this has reduced itself to a nice gooey mixture, season with salt and pepper and add a touch of tomato purée if liked.

Stuffed Pancakes with Florentine Filling

Cook a large packet of frozen chopped spinach, toss in butter and season with salt, pepper and nutmeg. If there's any cream handy, add a little of that too.

Stuffed Pancakes with Mushroom Filling

Wash and slice $\frac{1}{2}$ lb. button mushrooms and sauté in a little butter until tender, then add $\frac{1}{2}$ tsp. flour to take up excess liquid, 2 tbs. cream, and season with salt, pepper and nutmeg.

Stuffed Pancakes with Red Pimento Filling

Sauté an onion and a crushed clove of garlic in butter, and when transparent add the chopped contents of a can of red peppers, and four skinned and sliced tomatoes. Flavour with a touch of basil, salt and pepper.

Sweetcorn Fritters

3 eggs	1 oz. flour
salt and pepper	11½ oz. can sweetcorn
1 tbs. lemon juice	1 clove garlic, crushed
2 tbs. vegetable oil	lemon and parsley to
8 oz. cottage cheese	garnish

Break eggs into liquidiser goblet, add salt and pepper, lemon juice and vegetable oil and liquidise until smooth, then add cottage cheese and flour, and liquidise again to make a thick, smooth mixture. Drain sweetcorn and stir into the mixture with the crushed garlic. Drop tablespoonfuls into hot deep fat and fry until golden and crisp. Drain on kitchen paper and serve piled up on a warm serving dish and garnished with lemon slices and parsley sprigs. Good with tomato sauce, p. 157.

Variations

Asparagus Fritters

Are very good, using canned asparagus instead of sweetcorn.

Artichoke Heart Fritters

Using canned artichoke hearts.

Okra Fritters

Using canned okra – serve these with curry sauce, p. 154 or p. 155.

Salsify Fritters

(Using canned or fresh cooked salsify) are delicious with lemon sauce, p. 156.

Cucumber Fritters

Skin, slice and steam a cucumber until tender, then drain and add to batter mixture; very good and delicate, nice with sauce tartare, p. 153.

Pasta

Many people avoid serving pasta since they feel it is too fattening. However it is quick, filling and appetising, and if served with a simple green salad or watercress and followed by fresh fruit, the meal may well contain fewer calories than many other cooked meals. A well-balanced meal of pasta is therefore well worth considering, and is especially useful as a quickly prepared meal for unexpected guests. Wholemeal pasta obtainable from health food stores can be used in all the following recipes except the quick macaroni cheese where quick macaroni is used. Any number of different vegetables can be added to the cooked macaroni or spaghetti, and protein can be provided in the meal by serving the pasta with a cheese sauce or with a generous garnish of grated or toasted flaked nuts, or a good bowlful of freshly grated cheese or with a generous garnish of sliced hardboiled egg or by incorporating these into the actual savoury. All the recipes in this section are quickly made, and all can be infinitely varied according to what there is in the storecupboard.

Macaroni with Celery and Mushrooms

1 head celery or 16 oz. can celery hearts	dash yeast extract
8 oz. macaroni	salt and pepper
1 large onion	chopped parsley and tomato slices to garnish
1½ tbs. vegetable oil	8 oz. grated cheese
8 oz. mushroom stalks	

If using fresh celery, wash and chop and cook in a little boiling water till tender; if using canned, drain, chop and heat. Cook macaroni as directed on packet; drain and keep warm. While macaroni is cooking, fry peeled and chopped onion gently in the oil until tender. Add washed and chopped mushroom stalks, a very little

97

yeast extract, celery and drained macaroni. Season and heat through. Serve on a hot plate, surrounded with grated cheese, and garnished with chopped parsley and sliced tomatoes. Serve with green salad or spinach.

Variation

Creamy Macaroni with Celery and Mushrooms

For an extra rich and creamy dish, make as above but stir in 8 oz. cream cheese just before serving.

Macaroni with Peppers

8 oz. macaroni	1 can okra (optional)
2 large onions	salt and pepper
1½ tbs. vegetable oil	8 oz. grated cheese
1 large green pepper	garnish – a few black olives,
1 large red pepper	if available, chopped parsley
4 tomatoes, sliced	

Cook the macaroni in plenty of fast-boiling water as directed on packet. When just tender drain and keep warm. Meanwhile peel and slice onions and cook gently in the oil with the lid on the pan for 5 minutes. Wash, de-seed and slice peppers and add to onions. Continue to cook with lid on pan until vegetables are all just tender, then add tomatoes and okra if using. Add macaroni, season and heat through. Serve on a hot plate surrounded by grated cheese, and sprinkled with black olives and chopped parsley.

A good quick supper dish served with watercress or green salad, and followed with fresh fruit or water ice.

Macaroni Cheese

6–8 oz. macaroni	4 oz. grated cheese
4 oz. cream cheese	breadcrumbs for topping

Cook macaroni in fast-boiling salted water until tender; drain, add cream cheese and 2 oz. of the grated cheese, and stir over a gentle heat until cheeses melt. Top with breadcrumbs and the rest of the grated cheese and brown under grill. Very quick to make.

Macaroni Casserole

2 onions	14 oz. can tomatoes
1 oz. margarine	8 oz. grated cheese
8 oz. macaroni	cornflakes for topping

Peel, chop and fry onions in the margarine for 10 minutes. In a deep ovenproof dish arrange layers of onion, uncooked macaroni, the tomatoes with their liquid and all but 2 tbs. of the cheese. Top with cornflakes and the rest of the grated cheese, and bake in a moderate oven, at 325 °F., gas mark 3, for 1 hour.

This is a handy savoury because it can be left in a pre-set oven.

Spaghetti with Aubergine

1 large aubergine	$\frac{1}{2}$ lb. ripe tomatoes
1 onion, sliced	1 wine glass white wine
1 clove garlic, crushed	(optional)
3 tbs. olive oil	salt and pepper
oregano or basil	cooked spaghetti or
1 green pepper, sliced	tagliatelli
	grated parmesan cheese

Slice aubergine, salt lightly and leave for about $\frac{1}{2}$ hour, then drain and dry. Sauté onion and garlic in the oil for a few minutes, then add the aubergine and sauté a while longer until turning colour. Add herbs, sliced pepper and tomatoes and cook for a further 10 minutes. If wine is desired, add 1 wine glass of white wine and cook for another 5 minutes. Arrange cooked spaghetti or tagliatelli on a warm serving dish; pour the aubergine mixture into the centre, and scatter with parmesan cheese.

Spaghetti Milanese

4 oz. mushrooms	water – see recipe
1 onion	salt and pepper
½ oz. margarine	8 oz. spaghetti
1 small can tomato purée	½ oz. butter
1½ oz. ham flavour protoveg	grated parmesan cheese

Cook sliced mushrooms and onion in the margarine for a few minutes, then add tomato purée and the ham protoveg, hydrated as explained on p. 146. Cook for a few minutes, stirring all the time, then add enough water to make a sauce, and simmer gently for 15 minutes. Season to taste with salt and pepper.

Meanwhile cook spaghetti in boiling water with a little salt for 12 minutes. Spaghetti should be nearly soft. Drain and add ½ oz. butter. Serve with the sauce poured over, and hand round grated parmesan cheese.

Pastries and Pizza

In these recipes, pastries combine with vegetables, cheese and other proteins to make substantial meals. The pizza is particularly quick and easy to make.

All the recipes are planned for 100 per cent wholemeal plain flour, which adds an interesting texture and nutty flavour to the dishes. Recipes for the pastries used are in Chapter V.

Asparagus Quiche

6 oz. shortcrust pastry	2 eggs
1 small can asparagus tips	salt and pepper
½ pint top milk, evaporated milk or single cream	1 tbs. chopped parsley
	1–2 oz. finely grated cheese (optional)

Line flan case with shortcrust pastry, prick bottom, cover with a circle of greaseproof and dried beans, and bake for 10 minutes in a fairly hot oven, 400 °F., gas mark 6. Remove beans and greaseproof from flan case and bake for a further 5 minutes with oven turned down to moderate, 375 °F., gas mark 3. Meanwhile drain and chop asparagus, reserving 4 'best' pieces for decoration. Beat eggs with the cream or top milk, season to taste, add parsley. Put asparagus and grated cheese in flan case; pour in the egg mixture, and arrange the reserved asparagus on top. Return to the moderate oven for 35 minutes until set. Serve hot with cooked vegetables, or cold with salad.

Aubergine and Tomato Quiche

6 oz. cottage cheese pastry, p. 182	4 tomatoes, sliced
	$\frac{1}{4}$ pint stock
1 aubergine (about 8 oz.)	1 tbs. chopped parsley
1 clove garlic, crushed	2 eggs
2 tbs. vegetable oil	salt and pepper

Line flan case with cottage cheese pastry; cook as for Asparagus Quiche. Dice aubergine into $\frac{1}{4}''$ pieces, sprinkle with salt, leave for 30 minutes, then squeeze out moisture. Fry aubergine with crushed garlic in the oil for 10 minutes, add tomatoes and stock and cook for a further 5 minutes. Add parsley, beaten eggs and seasoning. Mix well; pour into flan case, bake in a slow oven at 300 °F., gas mark 2, for 35 minutes until set. Serve hot with cooked vegetables, or cold with salad.

If there isn't time to let aubergine stand in salt for 30 minutes, it can be diced and cooked straightaway. It can be a little bitter if not salted first, but personally I do not always bother with the salting if aubergine is to be sliced or diced and fried.

Quiche Florentine

6 oz. shortcrust pastry	4 oz. cottage or cream cheese
4 oz. packet frozen chopped spinach	salt, pepper and nutmeg
	2 eggs, beaten
good knob of butter	1–2 oz. grated parmesan cheese

Use pastry to line flan tin or dish. Prick bottom and bake as for Asparagus Quiche. Meanwhile, thaw spinach by steaming it first until softened, then toss it in the melted butter. Remove from heat and mix in cottage cheese (for an extra smooth texture, sieve in). Season with salt, pepper and nutmeg; beat in eggs. Turn into flan case, smooth top and sprinkle with the grated parmesan cheese. Return to oven, turn heat down to 325 °F., gas mark 3, and cook for 30–40 minutes. Serve hot or cold.

For a particularly decorative effect, strips of canned red pepper can be criss-crossed on top of half-cooked flan.

Sweetcorn Soufflé Quiche

8 oz. shortcrust pastry	1 oz. 81 per cent flour or white flour
11½ oz. can sweetcorn	
just under ½ pint milk	2 eggs, separated
1 oz. butter	salt, pepper and paprika
	1–2 oz. grated cheese

Use pastry to line a 9″ flan dish; lightly prick bottom and bake as for Asparagus Quiche.

Drain sweetcorn and make the liquid up to ½ pint with milk. Make a roux by melting the butter and stirring in the flour to make a smooth paste; remove from heat to stir in the milk, then stir over a gentle heat until thickened. Add egg yolks, sweetcorn and seasoning; whip whites stiffly and fold into mixture. Spoon into flan case, scatter with grated cheese and bake in the preheated oven at 375 °F., gas mark 5, for 25 minutes until risen and golden. This is delicious hot or cold.

Variation

Asparagus Soufflé Quiche

Is made in exactly the same way, using a can of green asparagus, chopped, instead of the sweetcorn.

Mushroom and Egg Pasties

filling:
2 oz. butter
4 oz. sliced mushrooms
2 oz. 81 per cent
   wholemeal flour
$\frac{3}{4}$ pint milk
4 hardboiled eggs
salt, pepper and mace
1 tbs. chopped parsley

wholemeal shortcrust:
6 oz. plain 100 per cent
   wholemeal flour
6 oz. plain 81 per cent
   wholemeal flour
$1\frac{1}{2}$ level tsp. baking powder
3 oz. vegetable margarine
3 oz. white vegetable fat
3 tbs. cold water
1 raw egg, beaten with
   $\frac{1}{2}$ tsp. salt, to glaze

Start by making the filling, as this must get cold before using. Melt butter and lightly sauté the mushrooms until tender, then add flour – I always use an 81 per cent flour for sauces as it is more glutinous than 100 per cent and more nutritious than cornflour. When mixture froths, draw off heat and add milk. Return to heat and stir until thickened; simmer for 10 minutes to cook flour, then add hardboiled eggs, finely chopped, salt, pepper and mace to taste, and parsley. Leave to get quite cold, while making pastry.

Normally for pastry I use all 100 per cent wholemeal flour, but since this can be a bit of a thing to make until you're used to it, because it is much more crumbly than white pastry, for this particular recipe which necessitates the folding over of the pastry into pasties, I think it wisest to start with a mixture of 100 per cent and 81 per cent or white flour until the texture is familiar.

Sift together the flours and baking powder – this, by the way, is necessary to give a really light result with wholemeal flour – there will be a residue of bran left in the sieve – add this to the sifted flour. Rub in the margarine and vegetable fat as usual, then add the water to bind and gather into a ball. Divide into 8 pieces, and roll each out, cutting it into a 6″ round using a saucer as a guide. Place a good heap of the filling on each, damp edges and gather up sides to centre, cornish pasty style. Brush with the beaten egg (the addition of salt gives a really shiny glaze), and bake at 425 °F., gas mark 7, for 20 minutes until golden and crisp.

This recipe can be varied by using chopped canned asparagus to make *asparagus and egg pasties*, or cooked, chopped leeks for *leek and egg pasties*; *pimento and egg pasties* are good too, using canned red peppers.

Wholemeal pastry has a nutty flavour and texture which contrasts well with the creamy filling and makes white pastry taste like old cardboard by comparison.

Quick Pizza

8 oz. flour	$\frac{1}{2}$ tsp. marjoram or oregano
2 tsp. baking powder	6 tomatoes
$\frac{1}{4}$ pint + 2 tbs. milk	6 oz. bel paese cheese
vegetable oil	8 olives
3 large onions	salt and pepper

Sift flour and baking powder into large bowl. Make a well in the centre and pour in milk. Mix quickly, then turn out of bowl and knead into two rounds. Place each on a baking sheet, press out to a depth of $\frac{1}{2}$″ and brush well with oil.

Slice onions and fry in oil with the herbs. Divide between two pizzas. Slice tomatoes into rings and place on top of onions. Slice cheese thinly and arrange over top. Be sure to take filling right to edges of pizzas. Halve olives and scatter over cheese. Drop a very little oil over top; season lightly with salt and pepper; bake in a hot oven at 450 °F., gas mark 8, for 20 minutes, until crisp and golden. Eat while still hot with tossed green salad.

Savoury Chutney Roll

8 oz. shortcrust pastry, p. 181
1 onion
2 tbs. vegetable oil
10 oz. can nuttolene
3 tbs. sweet chutney such as Marigold basil chutney
salt and pepper
1 beaten egg

Roll the shortcrust into a large oval. Peel, chop and fry the onion in oil until tender. Dice the nuttolene, then mix all the ingredients together, season well. Place the savoury mixture on one half of the pastry and fold over to form a pasty shape. Moisten edges of the pastry with cold water and press together. Brush with beaten egg and bake in a fairly hot oven, 400 °F., gas mark 6, for 25 minutes. Serve hot with brown sauce, or cold in slices with a salad.

Savoury Pie

1 tbs. vegetable oil
1 large onion, chopped
$\frac{1}{4}$ lb. mushrooms, washed and chopped
$1\frac{1}{2}$ tbs. flour
approx. $\frac{1}{2}$ pint stock
yeast extract
salt and pepper
1 small can meatless steaks, chopped
$\frac{1}{2}$ small can nuttolene, chopped
8 oz. shortcrust pastry

Heat oil and fry onion for 10 minutes until soft but not brown; then add the mushrooms, cook for a further 5 minutes, and then sprinkle on the flour and add the stock, made up to $\frac{1}{2}$ pint with the liquid strained from the meatless steaks. Season with yeast extract, salt and pepper. Make the pastry and use one half of it to line a deep ovenproof dish. Pour mushroom mixture into the pastry-lined ovenproof dish, add chopped steaks and nuttolene and top with the other half of pastry. Prick top and bake at 450 °F., gas mark 8, for 20 minutes.

Pulse Dishes

The dried beans and lentils are a wonderful source of nourishment, particularly in the winter, and though, granted, they can be dull, with clever flavouring and an imaginative touch they can also be most tasty and warming. They are a very economical source of protein, and also rich in iron and other minerals.

Most pulses benefit from an overnight soak: cover them generously with boiling water, and leave. Next day, cook gently, in the same water – if you strain it away you also lose valuable minerals – until really tender. This takes about $\frac{1}{2}$ hour or less in the case of lentils, 2 hours for butterbeans and haricots; and about 4 hours for soya beans. Pulses can be soaked and cooked and kept for at least a week in the fridge or for some months in the deep-freeze ready for speedy use in any of the following recipes.

Butterbeans à la Crême

4 oz. butterbeans	2 heaped tbs. flour
$\frac{1}{2}$ lemon	1 pint milk
1 onion	2 heaped tbs. chopped parsley
2 oz. margarine or butter	salt and pepper
	croûtons to decorate

Presoak butterbeans and cook as described until tender, then drain and preferably strip off transparent skins. Sprinkle with lemon and season with salt and pepper. Keep warm in an ovenproof serving dish. Peel and chop onion finely and stew gently in the margarine or butter until tender but not browned, then add the flour, mix well, remove from heat and add milk. Return to heat to thicken and simmer for 10 minutes. Then add parsley and seasoning and pour over butterbeans. Serve very hot, garnished with croûtons to give the necessary texture contrast.

Butterbean Curry

6 oz. butterbeans	2″ piece cinnamon
1 large onion	1 chilli
6 tbs. vegetable oil	2 tbs. flour
1 tsp. ground cumin	1 pint water
2 tsp. ground coriander	4 tomatoes, skinned and
2″ piece stem ginger	chopped
2 cloves	salt and pepper

Soak butterbeans overnight, then cook until tender. Chop onion and fry gently in the vegetable oil until tender; then add the spices and chopped ginger and cook for a couple of minutes before stirring in the flour, water and tomatoes and simmering for 10 minutes. Remove piece of cinnamon. Season with salt and pepper and serve with boiled rice and a tossed salad.

Butterbean Croquettes

4 oz. dried butterbeans or	1 tsp. grated lemon rind
15½ oz. can butterbeans	pinch sage
1 onion	salt and pepper
1 tbs. vegetable oil	1 egg, beaten
1 tbs. lemon juice	4 oz. fresh breadcrumbs

Soak and cook butterbeans as described. Drain (liquid is not needed) and mash. Finely chop onion and sauté in the oil for 15 minutes. Add to butterbeans with lemon juice and rind, sage, seasoning, beaten egg and fresh breadcrumbs. Check seasoning. Form into croquettes, coat with flour and shallow fry until crisp. Serve with red currant jelly, sauce espagnole, tomato sauce or English curry sauce.

Dhal

2 cups of red lentils	$\frac{1}{2}$ tsp. ginger
$4\frac{1}{2}$ cups water	$\frac{1}{2}$ tsp. turmeric
1 bayleaf	2 tbs. oil
2 medium onions, sliced	2 tsp. garam masala
2 cloves garlic, crushed	salt and pepper

Soak lentils in the water overnight, then simmer gently with the bayleaf, half the onions and half the garlic, the ginger, and turmeric until tender – about half an hour. Meanwhile fry the rest of the onion and garlic in the oil until browned, add garam masala and pour the mixture into the lentils. Stir and leave for at least 10 minutes (or as long as possible) for flavours to blend. Better still, leave overnight, reheat and serve piping hot with rice.

Dhal with Green Peppers and Bananas

dhal, made as above	3 bananas
1 large green pepper	1 carton sour cream

Make dhal as above, but fry sliced pepper with the onion. Just before serving, add the peeled and sliced bananas to the mixture, and stir in the sour cream.

Dhal with Red Peppers and Sour Cream

dhal, made as above	1 carton sour cream
$6\frac{1}{2}$ oz. can red peppers	chopped chives
4 tomatoes	

Make dhal as above, add red peppers, roughly chopped, and tomatoes, skinned and sliced. Reheat; spoon on to a serving dish, top with sour cream and a good scattering of chopped chives.

Dhal and Mixed Vegetables

1 large onion	few peas or green beans
2 tbs. oil	3 tomatoes
1 very small cauliflower	dhal, made as above

Slice onion and fry in the oil until tender and lightly browned. Break cauliflower into florets and cook in a little boiling water until just tender. The faster cooking peas or beans can be added to same pan during cooking time to finish with cauliflower. Drain vegetables, skin and slice tomatoes. Add all vegetables to dhal – serve very hot. Of course other combinations of vegetables can be used, according to what is to hand.

Lentil Curry English Style

8 oz. lentils	1–2 tbs. oil
1 bayleaf	1 tbs. curry powder
1 large onion	3 heaped tbs. sultanas
1 small apple	salt and pepper
1 clove garlic	squeeze lemon juice
	$\frac{1}{2}$ small cucumber, chopped

Soak lentils in 1 pint water for several hours; cook gently with bayleaf until soft. Meanwhile peel and chop onion and apple, crush garlic and fry all together in the oil with curry powder and sultanas for 15 minutes. Add lentils, salt, pepper and lemon juice to taste, and the cucumber. Serve with rice or creamed potatoes.

Lentils and Mushrooms au gratin

6 oz. lentils	salt and pepper
1 pint milk and water mixed	1 tsp. yeast extract
2 oz. butter	8 oz. mushrooms or mushroom stalks
1 large onion	1–2 oz. each of fresh
juice and rind of $\frac{1}{2}$ lemon	breadcrumbs and grated cheese for topping

Soak lentils in the liquid overnight or for a few hours if possible. Simmer in their liquid until golden and tender. Meanwhile melt half the butter, add peeled and sliced onion; cook until tender but not brown. Add to lentils, with lemon juice and grated or pared rind, salt, pepper and yeast extract; liquidise to make smooth, thick purée. Wash and slice mushrooms or mushroom stalks and fry in the rest of the butter until just tender. Place fried mushrooms in a shallow casserole; top with lentil mixture and the breadcrumbs and cheese. Bake in a moderate oven, 350 °F., gas mark 4, for 40–45 minutes, until golden and bubbly.

This is delicious served with sauce espagnole, p. 155, and a green vegetable, such as spinach – perhaps a few grilled tomatoes too?

Variations

Lentils and Celery au gratin

Is very tasty. Use the outside stalks of one large head of celery, chopped and cooked instead of mushrooms.

Lentils and Marrow au gratin

Using instead of mushrooms 1 lb. marrow, cubed, and lightly fried in butter and oil until tender.

Lentils and Tomatoes au gratin

Using 6 tomatoes, skinned and sliced, instead of mushrooms – a touch of basil is good with this.

Soya Bean and Sultana Curry

6 oz. soya beans	2 tbs. flour
1 large onion	water – see recipe
1 clove garlic	4 oz. sultanas
1 dessert apple	salt and pepper
2 tbs. oil	lemon juice
1 level desstsp. curry powder	sugar to taste

Soak soya beans overnight – or for 24 hours if possible – then cook slowly for 4 hours, or until really tender. Strain off liquid and use; make up to $\frac{3}{4}$ pint with water, to make the curry. Chop onion finely, crush garlic, chop apple and fry in the oil with the curry powder until tender. Then add the flour, mix well, and add the water, sultanas and soya beans. Simmer gently for 15–20 minutes, then season carefully and serve with mango chutney, creamed potatoes or boiled rice, and a tossed green salad.

Haricots can be used instead of soya beans in this curry but are not as rich in protein.

Rice Dishes

Quick, tasty and often complete in themselves – with perhaps watercress or a tossed salad – rice dishes are a wonderful standby for speedy meals, as well as being fairly foolproof meals for entertaining.

Long grain natural rice can be obtained from health food stores; it looks like rather dirty ordinary rice and takes longer to cook, but has much more flavour and nutritive value than the polished grain and, when cooked, is a great deal whiter than its dry state would lead one to believe.

Brown or unpolished rice contains some protein and is a fine food, rich in vitamins and minerals. For a balanced meal however, extra protein needs to be added either to the actual savoury or as an accompaniment such as hard-boiled egg slices or grated cheese. Another way of adding protein to a rice meal is to serve omelette shreds. For these, allow an egg per person; make one or more omelettes then roll them up and cut into shreds, as fine or thick as you like. Or omelettes can be cut into ribbons which can be criss-crossed decoratively over the top of savouries, making a protein-rich garnish. Roasted nuts also go very well with rice, adding texture; they can be added to a dish or served as a garnish.

For special occasions, rice dishes such as the aubergines with rice, the various pilau, the paëlla or the fried rice, can be made especially attractive by pressing mixture into a well-oiled ring mould. Keep warm in oven until ready to serve, then turn out on to a warm dish, fill centre of ring with sliced tomatoes or lightly fried button mushrooms or roasted nuts or sliced hard-boiled egg, perhaps lightly bound with a good sauce, see p. 152, or watercress or spring onions, or anything else which will contrast well with the rice and make an attractive addition to the meal.

To cook, wash rice carefully in several waters, picking out loose floating husks and hard bits. Cover with about 1″ of cold salted water, bring to the boil and cook gently until soft, and all the water is absorbed. With unpolished rice this usually takes about $\frac{1}{2}$ hour.

Chinese Fried Rice

1 large onion	1 can bean sprouts
1 green pepper	1 can bamboo shoots
1 clove garlic	2 tbs. oil
1 piece preserved stem ginger	12 oz. cooked rice (this is about 4 oz. uncooked rice)
$\frac{1}{4}$ fresh pineapple or 8 oz. can pineapple chunks	1 tbs. soy sauce
	salt and pepper
8 oz. mushrooms	omelette shreds, p. 111, or 4–6 oz. blanched almonds

Chop onion and pepper; very finely chop or crush garlic and ginger; roughly chop pineapple chunks and mushrooms. Drain bean sprouts and bamboo shoots. Heat oil and toss in all vegetables, fry over a high heat for 3 minutes, stirring all the time. Add rice, soy sauce, and salt and pepper. Keep over heat until rice is really hot. Add blanched almonds if using, or make omelette shreds, p. 111. Pile rice mixture on serving dish; scatter with omelette shreds, if using, and serve. Can be accompanied by sweet-sour sauce if liked.

Anything can go into this; it is the preparation, cooking and flavouring which gives Chinese food its distinction, rather than the ingredients, which are for the

most part very similar to our western ones. It is a style of
cooking ideally suited to vegetarian ingredients. I look
in the fridge hopefully and use what ingredients come to
hand; for an everyday meal the bean sprouts and bamboo shoots can even be omitted. Cabbage, carrots and
celery can all be included, but must be well cut up as the
cooking time is short.

Egg and Mushroom Pilau

8 oz. natural rice	1 bayleaf
2 oz. butter	6 oz. button mushrooms
1 onion	salt and pepper
1 clove garlic	4 hardboiled eggs
1 tsp. curry powder	2 oz. toasted flaked almonds
$\frac{1}{2}$ tsp. turmeric	$\frac{1}{2}$ green pepper, chopped
1 tsp. cardamoms	2 oz. raisins

Cook rice in plenty of boiling water until tender, then
drain. Meanwhile melt butter and fry chopped onion and
crushed garlic with curry powder, turmeric, cardamoms
and bayleaf for 10 minutes until golden. Add the mushrooms and cook for a minute or two longer, then mix in
the drained rice, chopped hardboiled eggs, almonds,
chopped green pepper and raisins. Serve with curry
sauce.

Variations

Egg and Okra Pilau

Is made by omitting mushrooms and adding 15 oz.
can of okra instead.

Egg and Pea Pilau

Use 4 oz. frozen peas instead of the button mushrooms
– cook according to the directions on packet – and add
with the rice.

Fried Rice

1 cup long grain rice	3 cloves
1½ tbs. oil	1 bayleaf
¾ tsp. turmeric	salt and pepper

Wash rice thoroughly; drain and leave for a bit to dry. Fry the rice in oil over a gentle heat until rice has become opaque or white, do *not* brown. Stir all the time, that is, for about 5 minutes or so, which is a bit of a bore but worth it. Have ready a kettle of boiling water. Pour on to rice *just* covering it (about 2 cups), add turmeric, cloves, bayleaf, salt and pepper. Put on lid tightly, turn heat down very, very low or put container into a low oven and cook for about 30 minutes. Rice should be dry and in separate grains, serve with curries.

Kebabs

½ green pepper	*basting sauce:*
8 oz. button mushrooms	1 tsp. dry mustard
8 oz. can pineapple chunks	1 tbs. red currant jelly
½ cucumber, skinned	1 tbs. vinegar
10 oz. can nuttolene or	1 tbs. tomato ketchup
meatless steaks or	6 tbs. oil
4–6 hardboiled eggs	salt and pepper
4 tomatoes	boiled rice to serve

Cut pepper into slivers, removing seeds and pith. Wash mushrooms, halving any really big ones. Cover both with boiling water and leave for 3–4 minutes, then drain and rinse under cold water. Drain pineapple. Slice cucumber and nuttolene or meatless steaks, whichever you are using, into chunky pieces or quarter eggs, also tomatoes. Thread pieces of green pepper, mushroom, pineapple, tomato and nuttolene, meatless steaks or egg, on to skewers, continuing until skewers are full. Brush thoroughly with a sauce made by blending together the mustard, red currant jelly, vinegar, tomato ketchup and oil. Sprinkle with salt and pepper, and place under a moderately hot grill, basting and turning from time to time, for about 20 minutes, until vegetables are cooked. Serve on a bed of boiled rice.

For a special presentation, hot boiled rice can be pressed into an oiled ring mould and turned on to a warm plate, and the kebabs placed in centre of ring. Or, try seasoning the rice with fried onion, or colouring it with a little turmeric, or adding raisins or sweetcorn to it . . . the variations are endless. All-vegetable kebabs served with a savoury rice containing nut or egg for protein are delicious and satisfying.

Paëlla – vegetarian style

2 large aubergines	$\frac{1}{2}$ lb. button mushrooms
8 oz. natural rice	juice of 1 lemon
2 large onions	8 tomatoes, skinned and
1 clove garlic	quartered
4 tbs. vegetable oil	4–6 oz. flaked almonds,
2 bayleaves	toasted in moderate oven
1 red pepper	or under grill

Dice aubergines, sprinkle with salt and leave for $\frac{1}{2}$ hour. Meanwhile cook rice in plenty of boiling water until tender, then drain; rinse under cold water, then keep warm. Chop onions and garlic and sauté gently in the oil with the bayleaves for 10 minutes. Drain off and discard the liquor which the aubergines will have produced, and add the aubergines to the onions with the pepper, de-seeded and sliced and the mushrooms. Cook for a few minutes more, then add rice, lemon juice and seasoning, using a fork to mix to avoid mashing the vegetables. Just before serving add the tomatoes and almonds.

I know that this is a slightly unconventional way of making a rice and vegetable dish, but I find that by cooking the vegetables separately from the rice they can be cooked each perfectly, making a better result.

Rice and Cheese Loaf

8 oz. rice	2 tomatoes
4–6 oz. grated cheese	2 eggs, beaten
4 oz. pkt. mixed frozen vegetables	salt and pepper
	pinch saffron or turmeric (optional)
1 large onion	lemon slices ⎫
2 cloves garlic	
2 tbs. oil	1 tbs. chopped ⎬ for garnish
6½ oz. can red peppers (optional)	parsley ⎭

Cook rice in plenty of boiling water until just tender. Cook mixed frozen vegetables according to directions on packet, drain. Finely chop onion and crush garlic; sauté in 2 tbs. oil for 5 minutes. If using peppers, chop finely, reserving one for garnish; skin and chop tomatoes. With a fork mix all ingredients together, and season, adding turmeric or saffron if using. Line 2 lb. loaf tin with buttered foil and fill with rice mixture. Cover with more foil and bake for 1 hour in a moderate oven, 350 °F., gas mark 4. Remove from tin carefully and peel off foil. Garnish with strips of red pepper, lemon slices and parsley. Serve with lemon sauce.

VEGETABLES

Many vegetable dishes which in a meat diet are normally served as subsidiaries to a main meat course are in fact delicious dishes in their own right. Others, when served with protein sauce or the addition of extra protein, can become main dishes. Vegetables in season make economical, tasty, healthy main dishes for everyday, while the more unusual vegetables make delicious special dishes and are a boon in the vegetarian diet, where, dare I say, they get the respect they deserve, forming the centre of the meal without competition from more strongly flavoured meats!

This section is divided into three: vegetable bakes and casseroles; stuffed vegetables, very delicious and popular; and 'top of the stove' vegetable dishes, many of them very quick and easy to make.

I do hope you will enjoy these dishes made from the most 'vital' foods of all – fresh vegetables, full of vitamins and minerals, not to mention flavour!

BAKES AND CASSEROLES
Croustade of Mushrooms

croustade:
4 oz. soft breadcrumbs
4 oz. ground almonds, or
  other nuts, finely milled
2 oz. butter or margarine
4 oz. flaked almonds,
  pinekernels or hazelnuts
1 clove garlic
½ tsp. mixed herbs

topping:
1 lb. mushrooms
2 oz. butter
2 heaped tbs. flour
¾ pint milk
salt, pepper and nutmeg
4 tomatoes
1 tbs. chopped parsley

First make croustade by mixing together breadcrumbs and ground almonds or other milled nuts. Rub in butter or margarine as for pastry. Add flaked almonds, or other nuts, chopped finely. If using hazelnuts, first prepare by baking on a dry baking sheet for 20–30 minutes at 350 °F., gas mark 4, until skins will rub off in a clean cloth. Crush garlic and add to nut mixture with mixed herbs; mix together well and then press down very firmly in a flat ovenproof dish or swiss roll tin. Bake in a hot oven, 450 °F., gas mark 8, for 15–17 minutes until crisp and golden brown. Meanwhile make topping. Wash and slice mushrooms; sauté in the butter until tender, then add the flour and when it froths, remove from heat and stir in the milk. Return to heat and stir until thickened, simmer for 10 minutes over a low heat, then season well with salt, pepper and nutmeg. Spoon mushroom mixture on top of croustade; top with tomatoes, skinned and sliced, and sprinkle with a very little salt and pepper. Return to oven for 10–15 minutes to heat through, then serve sprinkled with parsley.

This all sounds rather fiddly, but in fact it's very straightforward and the creamy topping is delicious with the crisp protein-rich croustade. Other vegetables can be used: *croustade of leeks*, *croustade of vegetable marrow* and *croustade of courgettes* are made in exactly the same way. *Croustade of aubergines* can also be made similarly, but it's best to salt the aubergine before using. I like to sauté a green or red pepper with the aubergine. For *croustade of okra* or *sweetcorn* or *asparagus* make the sauce as above, then add the drained contents of a large can of one of these vegetables. *Croustade of cauliflower* is another variation – use a medium-sized cauliflower, break into florets and steam or boil until tender before adding to the sauce – make *croustade of celery* similarly. Both these are nice with a few mushrooms added for extra flavour.

Timbale aux Marrons

¼ lb. dehydrated chestnuts	juice and rind ½ lemon
15½ oz. can unsweetened chestnut purée	4 oz. soft, fresh breadcrumbs
4 oz. melted butter	1 beaten egg
nutmeg and pepper	

Pour boiling water over the chestnuts, leave overnight; next day simmer until tender. Beat the canned chestnut purée until smooth, add the cooked chestnuts, melted butter and rest of ingredients. Spoon into foil-lined and buttered 1 lb. tin and bake at 375 °F., gas mark 5, for one hour. Turn out on to warm dish and remove foil. Looks very attractive surrounded by crisp roast potatoes and decorated with strips of canned red pepper, lemon and parsley.

I sometimes make double these quantities and use a foil-lined 2½ pint ring mould to make the timbale in – allowing a longer cooking time. When turned out, fill centre with one of the fillings given for Roulade aux Marrons below. Garnish with parsley and strips of red pepper. Serve with wine sauce p. 157, or sauce espagnole p. 155.

Roulade aux Marrons

8 oz. can unsweetened chestnut purée
4 eggs
salt, pepper and nutmeg
rind and juice of ½ lemon
1 tbs. finely grated onion
½ oz. melted butter

filling:
½ lb. button mushrooms
or 1 can pimentos
a little butter
½ tsp. flour
small carton double cream
salt and pepper

Beat chestnut purée until smooth; add egg yolks, salt, pepper and nutmeg, lemon rind and juice, onion and melted butter. Whisk egg whites until stiff but not dry and fold into mixture. Turn in to a swiss roll tin lined with foil and brushed thoroughly with oil or melted butter. Bake in a hot oven, 425 °F., gas mark 7, for 8–10 minutes, until it springs back when lightly touched. While the roulade is in the oven, make the filling: Wipe and slice the mushrooms, or drain and slice pimentos (whichever you are using). Sauté either lightly in a little butter for 5 minutes, then add the flour, stir for a moment and add the cream. Season with salt and pepper. Now turn the roulade on to a piece of greaseproof paper which has been lightly dusted with flour, peel off the foil, spread with the filling, and using the greaseproof underneath to help, roll up and slide on to a warm serving dish. Decorate with chopped parsley, strips of red pepper or mushrooms, and perhaps surround with some duchesse potatoes. Serve with wine sauce p. 157, or sauce espagnole p. 155.

Mushroom Bake

$\frac{1}{2}$ lb. mushroom stalks	1 small onion, grated
4 oz. butter	6 oz. grated cheese
1 lb. tomatoes,	juice and rind of $\frac{1}{2}$ lemon
8 oz. fresh breadcrumbs	salt and pepper

Wash, and slice mushroom stalks, then fry in 1 oz. of the butter for 10 minutes. Skin and slice tomatoes and leave on one side. Blend together the crumbs, onion, cheese, remaining butter and lemon rind, and press half of the mixture into the casserole; pour mushrooms on top of this and then the sliced tomatoes; season well with salt and pepper and the lemon juice. Roll out remaining crumb mixture and press on top. Bake in a moderately hot oven, 375 °F., gas mark 5, for 30 minutes. Serve from the dish with a good sauce.

Other vegetables and combinations of vegetables can be used – cooked *cauliflower* or *leeks*, for instance, instead of the mushrooms, or cooked *vegetable marrow* or *onions* or fried *aubergines*.

Mushroom Layer

8 oz. pkt. green beans	$4\frac{1}{2}$ oz. pkt. potato crisps
12 oz. button mushrooms	4 oz. flaked almonds
or mushroom stalks	6 oz. grated cheese
knob of butter	$10\frac{1}{2}$ oz. can mushroom soup

Cook beans in a little boiling water until tender; wash mushrooms or mushroom stalks and fry lightly in the butter for 10 minutes until tender. Place a layer of half the potato crisps in the bottom of a good-sized ovenproof dish – a pyrex one is ideal; cover with a layer of half each of the beans, mushrooms, almonds and grated cheese. Repeat, then pour over the mushroom soup, and place in a moderate oven, 350 °F., gas mark 4, for 30–40 minutes. Serve piping hot with grilled tomatoes and other vegetables in season.

Mushroom Layer can be speedily made from store-cupboard ingredients by using canned beans with canned button mushrooms or for a change, sweetcorn.

Mushroom Timbale

1 large onion	1 heaped tsp. mixed herbs
8 flat mushrooms	8 oz. finely grated cashewnuts
2 tomatoes, skinned	8 oz. soft breadcrumbs
2 oz. butter	2 eggs
1 tbs. flour	salt and pepper
$\frac{1}{2}$ pint water	to garnish:
1 tsp. yeast extract	1 tomato, sliced
	1 lemon, sliced
	a few sprigs parsley

If you have ever wondered what vegetarians eat for Christmas dinner, here is your answer. It is delicious, hot or cold. The cashewnuts can be grated in a liquidiser, coffee mill or the finest drum of an electric or hand rotary grater.

Peel onion and chop finely; wash and finely chop 4 of the mushrooms and slice tomatoes; sauté together gently in the butter for 10 minutes, then add the flour. Stir for a minute, then add the water, yeast extract and herbs. Stir until thickened, then add the rest of the ingredients. Line a 2 lb. loaf tin with foil, then brush thoroughly with melted butter. Place the remaining 4 mushrooms, black side down, in bottom of tin, spoon mixture on top, smooth over and cover with more buttered foil, tying securely with string. Steam for 2 hours. Cool for 2 minutes, then turn out of tin on to a large warm serving dish and remove foil. Surround with roast potatoes. Garnish top with a row of alternate slices of tomato and lemon, and some sprigs of parsley, and serve with sauce espagnole, p. 155, which is the vegetarian gravy.

Onion Timbale with Parsley Stuffing

1 pint milk	*stuffing:*
1 bayleaf	4 oz. soft brown bread
1 onion	2 oz. margarine
1 clove	1 good tbs. chopped parsley
3 oz. semolina	$\frac{1}{2}$ tsp. mixed herbs
4 oz. finely milled	1 tsp. lemon juice
cashewnuts	2 tsp. lemon rind
pinch mace	to garnish:
2 eggs	lemon slices
salt and pepper	parsley sprigs

Make the basic onion timbale mixture by heating together the milk, bayleaf and onion (with the clove stuck into it); bring to the boil, remove from heat and leave for 15 minutes, then remove bayleaf and onion. Reheat milk to boiling point, then gradually sprinkle in the semolina, stirring vigorously all the time to avoid lumps. Cook gently for 5 minutes until very thick, still stirring well. Add cashewnuts, milled in a liquidiser, fine electric grater or electric coffee mill, the mace, eggs – beat them in well – and salt and pepper. Make a good stuffing by blending together all the other ingredients as listed. Line a 2 lb. loaf tin with foil and butter generously, then place a layer of half the white mixture in the bottom; spread the stuffing evenly over this and finish with the rest of the white mixture. Cover with foil, and bake in a fairly hot oven, 400 °F., gas mark 6, for 45 minutes to 1 hour, until nicely set. Cool for a minute or two, then loosen edges of roast and turn out on to a warm plate. Garnish with parsley and lemon slices and surround with roast potatoes. Serve with sauce espagnole, p. 155.

Pimento and Chestnut Casserole

2 large onions	1 bayleaf
1 head celery	2 cans whole chestnuts
1 tbs. vegetable oil	2 tbs. flour
6½ oz. can red peppers	just under 1 pint red wine
4 tomatoes, or 1 small can tomatoes	salt and pepper

Finely slice onions and celery and sauté in the oil for 10 minutes, then add the peppers, drained and sliced, the tomatoes, peeled and quartered (drained if using canned ones), and the bayleaf. Drain chestnuts, reserving liquid. Toss chestnuts in the flour, then add to the pan together with any excess flour. I use a flame-proof casserole which can go over the hotplate as well as into the oven. Make the reserved chestnut liquid up to 1 pint with the red wine, add to casserole. Season with salt and pepper and bake at 350 °F., gas mark 4, for 45 minutes.

Any left-over red wine can be used for this – don't get any in specially.

Although chestnuts are delicious, and this casserole is always popular, it is not rich in protein, and this deficiency needs to be made up either in the first course or in the dessert.

Variations
Mushroom and Chestnut Casserole

If you want a change, try using ½ lb. button mushrooms, wiped and sliced, instead of the peppers.

Textured Vegetable Protein Casserole

For a complete change, this recipe can also be made deliciously, using 2–3 oz. marigold vegetarian meat or protoveg chunks, either natural or flavoured, to replace the chestnuts. Hydrate (see p. 146) before draining well and proceeding as above.

Tomato Pie

1 lb. creamy mashed potatoes	salt, pepper and nutmeg
8 oz. grated cheese	1 lb. tomatoes, skinned
1 small onion, grated	pinch basil
	knob of butter

Add grated cheese and small grated onion to the potatoes, mix well and season with salt, pepper and nutmeg. Spread half mixture in a shallow buttered casserole; smooth well to form base of pie. Slice tomatoes, mix with seasoning and basil, and spread over potato base. Season lightly, spread with rest of potato to cover. Rough-up with prongs of fork and dot with butter. Bake in a fairly hot oven at 400 °F., gas mark 6, for 30–40 minutes, until golden brown.

Other vegetables can be used instead of tomatoes.

Variations

Mushroom Pie

Use 8–12 oz. sliced and lightly fried button mushrooms.

Sweetcorn Pie

Use 11½ oz. can of sweetcorn.

Vegetable Pie

1 lb. potatoes	salt and pepper
2 onions	basil
1 lb. or 14 oz. can tomatoes	celery salt
½ pint cheese sauce	2 oz. butter or margarine
	2 tbs. grated cheese

Peel and thinly slice potatoes and cook in boiling water until tender. Peel and slice onions and tomatoes and arrange in layers with potato in a well greased shallow dish with cheese sauce and seasoning of salt and pepper, basil and celery salt between each layer. Finish with layer of potato. Sprinkle with grated cheese and butter (or margarine), cover and cook in a moderate oven, 350 °F., gas mark 4, for 45 minutes.

This is a good family dish which can be infinitely varied. Try adding layers of thinly sliced cheese to the pie, or omit tomatoes and instead use layers of the savoury filling given on p. 94. Serve with sauce espagnole, p. 155. Or use thinly sliced mushrooms with, or instead of, tomatoes. Or add layers of thinly sliced vegetarian canned savoury such as nuttolene or saviand and serve with sauce espagnole, p. 155, and plenty of chutney – the chutney by Marigold is delicious.

STUFFED VEGETABLES
Stuffed Aubergines

2 medium-sized aubergines	1 egg
4 oz. flaked almonds, pinekernels or chopped nuts	1 tsp. yeast extract
	1 tsp. chopped parsley
	salt and pepper
2 large onions	squeeze lemon juice
1 clove garlic	2 oz. fresh soft
1 oz. butter	breadcrumbs
1 bayleaf	3 oz. grated cheese
4 oz. button mushrooms	

Wipe aubergines, score around lightly lengthwise and place on a dry baking sheet. Bake in a moderate oven, 350 °F., gas mark 4, for 30 minutes, until flesh can be pierced easily through the score mark. Insert point of knife in score mark and slice aubergines in half. Scoop out flesh leaving the skins intact. Leave skins on one side. Chop flesh finely and reserve. Flaked almonds, pinekernels or other nuts, chopped, can be toasted in the oven on a dry baking sheet while aubergines are cooking. Chop onions and crush garlic, sauté together in the butter with the bayleaf for 5 minutes, then add washed and chopped mushrooms and cook for a further 5 minutes. Beat the egg with the yeast extract, add aubergine pulp, parsley, flaked almonds or pinekernels and mushroom mixture. Season with salt, pepper and lemon juice. Spoon mixture into aubergine shells, top with the grated cheese and breadcrumbs mixed together and return to moderate oven, 350 °F., gas mark 4, for 20 minutes, until golden and crisp.

Serve with onion, tomato, or wine sauce.

The best flavour and texture is obtained by baking the aubergines in advance, perhaps the day before while the oven is hot for something else.

Stuffed Aubergines Provençales

2 medium-sized aubergines	1 tsp. tomato purée
2 large onions	4 oz. grated parmesan cheese
1 clove garlic	1 beaten egg
2 tbs. oil	4 oz. flaked almonds
bayleaf	salt and pepper
4 tomatoes	a little lemon juice
8 large black olives	1–2 oz. fresh breadcrumbs
	to garnish: 1 tbs. chopped parsley

Wipe aubergines, score around lightly lengthwise and place on a dry baking sheet. Bake in a moderate oven, 350 °F., gas mark 4, for 30 minutes, until flesh can be pierced easily through score mark. Insert point of knife into score mark and slice aubergines in half. Scoop out flesh, leaving the skins intact and leave on one side. Chop flesh finely and reserve. (This can all be done in advance as suggested in previous recipe.) Chop onion and crush garlic in a little salt; sauté together in the oil with the bayleaf for 10 minutes, then remove from heat and add the tomatoes skinned and sliced, the black

126

olives, stoned and chopped, the tomato purée, half the grated cheese, the egg, the aubergine pulp and the flaked almonds. Mix well together and season with salt, pepper and lemon juice. Pile into aubergine skins. Place in buttered ovenware dish, scatter with the rest of the cheese and the fresh breadcrumbs and bake in a moderate oven, 350 °F., gas mark 4, for 20 minutes until golden. Scatter with chopped parsley. Serve with sauce espagnole, p. 155, or wine sauce, p. 157.

Cabbage with Pineapple Stuffing

1 hearty cabbage, approx. 2½–3 lbs.	15 oz. can pineapple pieces
1 large onion	6 oz. walnuts
3 tbs. vegetable oil	juice ½ lemon
4 oz. breadcrumbs	salt and pepper
3 tomatoes	1–2 tsp. soy sauce
	grated nutmeg

Prepare cabbage to take stuffing by cutting off any tough leaves and trimming bottom so that it stands steady. Scoop out inside (save to use later, cooked, or in salads) leaving about 1″ thickness around outside. Wash, boil for 10 minutes, drain 'shell' thus made, place in buttered casserole. Skin and chop onion, fry lightly in the oil until tender. Add breadcrumbs, tomatoes, skinned and sliced, pineapple, drained and lightly chopped, walnuts, milled or very finely chopped, and lemon juice. Mix well together, season with salt and pepper, soy sauce and nutmeg. Pile into cabbage 'shell'. Cover and bake for 1 hour at 350 °F., gas mark 4. Serve with creamed or baked potatoes and tomato sauce, if liked, p. 157, and another vegetable, such as peas or beans.

This is a lovely blend of flavours and the walnuts add not only texture but protein to the dish.

Stuffed Globe Artichokes

4 globe artichokes	2 tbs. chopped parsley
8 oz. white bread	rind and juice 1 lemon
1 small onion	6 oz. grated cheese
2 oz. butter	salt and pepper

Trim top and bottom of artichokes, removing any damaged outer leaves and topmost leaves to make a cavity for stuffing. Cook artichokes in boiling water until tender and a leaf will come off easily – takes about 45 minutes. Drain artichokes and cut out the inedible hairy 'choke' inside. Make stuffing by slicing bread roughly and soaking for a minute or two in warm water, then squeeze out moisture and break up bread. Chop onion and fry in the butter until transparent but not browned, add to bread with parsley, lemon juice and rind, most of the cheese, pepper and salt. Pack into artichokes, place them in a buttered casserole and top with the remaining cheese. Bake in a moderate oven, 350 °F., gas mark 4, for 20 minutes. Serve with melted butter and lemon, hollandaise sauce or green herb sauce, p. 152 onwards.

Stuffed Courgettes

4 large courgettes	4 tbs. flaked almonds
4 oz. white breadcrumbs	rind and juice of $\frac{1}{2}$ lemon
8 oz. cream cheese	salt and pepper

Parboil courgettes for 5 minutes, then slice in half lengthwise and scoop out centres. Place side by side in a well-buttered ovenproof dish. Mix together the breadcrumbs, cream cheese, flaked almonds, scooped out courgette centres, mashed, lemon juice and rind, salt and pepper. Pile into prepared courgettes and bake in a fairly hot oven, 375 °F., gas mark 5, for 45 minutes. Serve hot with lemon sauce, sauce aurore or parsley sauce. Supply extra protein to the meal in the dessert or starter courses.

Stuffed Courgettes Mornay

4 large courgettes	1 tbs. lemon juice
1 clove garlic	1 tsp. lemon rind, grated
4 tomatoes	2 tbs. chopped parsley
6 oz. button mushrooms	salt and pepper
1 oz. butter	1–2 oz. grated cheese
4 oz. breadcrumbs	to serve: $\frac{3}{4}$ pint cheese
	sauce, p. 153

Prepare courgettes as in previous recipe. Crush garlic, slice tomatoes and mushrooms, and sauté lightly in the butter until tender. Mix with half the breadcrumbs, the chopped courgette centres, the lemon juice and rind, parsley, salt and pepper. Pile into prepared courgettes, place in buttered shallow ovenproof dish, sprinkle with the rest of the breadcrumbs and the grated cheese. Pop into a moderate oven, 350 °F., gas mark 4, for 20 minutes. Serve with cheese sauce.

Variation

Stuffed Cucumber Mornay

1 large cucumber   stuffing as for stuffed
courgettes, above

Prepare cucumber by cutting into 3–4″ lengths, halving and scooping out seeds. Continue as for Stuffed Courgettes Mornay.

Stuffed Fennel

2 large fennel plants
crispy stuffing from marrow recipe, p. 130, or
cheese and olive, p. 132, or cream cheese
stuffing, p. 128

Wash and trim fennel plants, halve and scoop out centres (save for salads) and boil or steam the fennel 'cups' until tender. Fill with crispy stuffing or cheese and olive stuffing or cream cheese stuffing and bake in a moderate oven, 350 °F., gas mark 4, for 20 minutes. Serve with brown or lemon sauce.

Marrow with Crispy Stuffing

1 medium-sized vegetable marrow
6 oz. wholemeal breadcrumbs
6 oz. finely milled nuts – almonds, hazelnuts, brazilnuts, walnuts, or a mixture

4 tbs. vegetable oil
½ lb. button mushrooms
4 tomatoes, skinned
1 small onion, grated
salt and pepper
parsley and tomato slices to garnish

Parboil marrow for 5 minutes, then cut in half length-wise; scoop out inside flesh and seeds to leave a cavity for the stuffing. Fry breadcrumbs and milled nuts together in the oil until crisp and golden, then add mushrooms, sliced, and fry until cooked. Remove from heat, add chopped marrow flesh and seeds if tender, tomatoes, sliced, grated onion, salt and pepper. Spoon mixture on to the marrow pressing it together as you do so and piling up well. Bake in a moderate oven, 350 °F., gas mark 4, for 30 minutes, or until tender. Garnish with parsley and sliced tomato. Serve with sauce espagnole, p. 155.

Marrow with Parsley and Herb Stuffing

1 medium-sized vegetable marrow
4 oz. breadcrumbs
4 oz. finely milled nuts
6 tbs. vegetable oil
2 good tbs. chopped parsley

½ tsp. mixed herbs
1 egg
1 small onion, grated
rind and juice of ½ lemon
salt and pepper

Cut end off marrow and scoop out seeds. Parboil marrow for 5 minutes. Meanwhile, cover bread with warm water; leave for a moment then crumble into a bowl and blend in all the other ingredients to make stuffing. Drain parboiled marrow, fill with stuffing, place in a buttered ovenproof dish and cover with buttered greaseproof paper. Bake in a fairly hot oven, 400 °F.,

VEGETARIAN MAIN COURSE SAVOURIES

gas mark 6, for 45 minutes to 1 hour, or until marrow is tender. Serve with sauce espagnole, p. 155, and with some extra protein in the meal, perhaps a protein rich starter, see Chapter III, or a protein dessert, see Chapter V.

Stuffed Marrow Rings

1 medium-sized vegetable marrow	4 tomatoes
2 onions	1 tbs. tomato purée
2 tbs. vegetable oil	salt, pepper and sugar
1 bayleaf	1 tsp. lemon juice
10 oz. can nuttolene or tartex savoury roll	parsley

Peel the marrow and cut into rings, one for each person. Scoop out seeds. Slice onion and fry gently in the oil with the bayleaf until tender – 15 minutes. Dice the nuttolene or tartex savoury roll and quarter the tomatoes, then add both to the onions with the tomato purée. Season with salt, pepper, sugar and lemon juice. Heat some oil in a large baking tin, place the marrow rings in this and fill each with the onion mixture. Cover all with a piece of greaseproof paper and bake in a fairly hot oven, 400 °F., gas mark 6, for 1 hour. Scatter generously with parsley. Serve with gravy made by stirring a little flour into the juices in the baking dish and adding stock, yeast extract, tomato purée, and seasoning to taste.

Stuffed Mushrooms

12 large flat mushrooms	lemon twists or tomato slices to garnish
stuffing mixture as for Stuffed Courgettes or Marrow with Crispy Stuffing	

Remove and chop mushroom stalks. Fry mushroom caps lightly in butter, then place black side up, in a

131

casserole and pile stuffing on top. Pour a little liquid around mushrooms – cream, stock or water – and bake for 20–30 minutes. Decorate each with a lemon twist or tomato slice.

Stuffed Onions

4 large onions	a little stock or water
parsley and herb	butter for greasing
stuffing, p. 130, or	
crispy stuffing, p. 130	

Peel the onions and cut in half horizontally. Cook in boiling water until nearly tender, then scoop out the inside of the onion to make 'cups'. Fill the 'cups' with the stuffing and place in a buttered shallow casserole. Pour around a little of the water in which the onions were cooked and bake in a moderate oven, 350 °F., gas mark 4, for 45 minutes to 1 hour. Serve with sauce espagnole, p. 155. Alternatively, make Stuffed Onions Mornay, proceeding as for Stuffed Courgettes Mornay, p. 129.

Peppers with Olive Stuffing

2 very large red or	6 oz. grated cheese
green peppers	4 oz. stoned olives
1 small onion	1 tbs. chopped parsley
2 oz. butter	salt and pepper
8 oz. bread	few drops tabasco

Halve peppers lengthwise and remove seeds and core, simmer in a little water for 5 minutes – drain. Meanwhile chop onion and sauté lightly in the butter until tender. Slice bread roughly, cover with warm water and leave for a minute to soften. Squeeze out water and crumble bread. Mix with the grated cheese, fried onion, stoned olives, parsley, salt, pepper and seasonings. Place pepper in halves in a buttered casserole. Fill with olive stuffing and bake at 350 °F., gas mark 4, for 45 minutes until golden, and peppers soft.

Other stuffings can be used; the crispy stuffing given for marrow is particularly good.

Stuffed Tomatoes

8 large tomatoes	crispy stuffing from marrow recipe, p. 130

Cut tops off tomatoes, scoop out pulp. Prepare stuffing using the scooped-out tomato centres instead of the tomatoes stated in stuffing recipe, p. 130. Pile mixture into tomatoes; replace 'lids' and bake in a moderate oven, 350 °F., gas mark 4, for 15–20 minutes.

Serve with sauce espagnole, p. 155.

Stuffed Vine Leaves

8 vine leaves	juice of $\frac{1}{2}$ lemon
2 oz. rice	1 egg, beaten
1 small onion	salt and pepper
1 clove garlic, crushed	6 oz. grated cheese
1 tbs. tomato purée	

Wash the vine leaves and blanch by pouring boiling water over them and leave for 1 minute. Drain. Boil the rice until tender and rinse under cold water. Meanwhile peel, chop and fry onion and crushed garlic, add tomato purée, rice, lemon juice, beaten egg, salt, pepper and half the cheese. Place spoonfuls of mixture on vine leaves and roll up. Place in an oiled casserole, scatter with rest of cheese and bake in a moderate oven, 350 °F., gas mark 4, for about half an hour. Serve with tomato sauce, p. 157.

Top-of-the-Stove Vegetable Dishes

Aubergines au Gratin

1½ lb. aubergines	1 desstsp. flour
vegetable oil	15 oz. can tomatoes
1 onion	salt, pepper and sugar to taste
1 clove garlic	4 oz. grated cheese

Wash aubergines, but do not peel. Slice into ½″ rounds, sprinkle with salt and leave for 30 minutes, then squeeze out bitter juice and fry the aubergines in a little oil until tender. Keep warm while preparing the sauce. To make this, chop onion and crush garlic and fry both in a little oil until tender; then add flour and cook for two minutes. Mash tomatoes and add to flour and oil; return to heat until thickened. Season with salt, pepper and sugar and simmer for a further 10 minutes to cook flour. Arrange aubergine slices in a large, flat casserole; pour tomato sauce over and top with grated cheese; brown under a moderate grill and serve piping hot.

Many other vegetables can be served in this way. Make *courgette*, *leek*, *mushroom* and *vegetable marrow au gratin* in exactly the same way; sauté the vegetables until tender in each case. For *cabbage*, *celery* or *potatoes* (yes, potatoes) *au gratin*, boil the vegetable concerned first, then toss in a little butter and cover with the sauce. For *sweetcorn au gratin*, either use fresh sweetcorn, cooked and then scraped from the husks, or use the contents of a couple of large cans, drained, and tossed in melted butter. *Butterbeans au gratin* are also surprisingly good: soak butterbeans overnight and cook until tender – see p. 106.

Celery Amandine

2 celery, chopped into
    bite-sized pieces
salt and pepper
2 oz. butter
2 tbs. chopped onion

a little flour
½ pint single cream
a dash of stock
8 oz. toasted flaked
    almonds
duchesse potato to serve

Cook celery, seasoning, lump of butter and onion over a low flame for 20 minutes or so in a covered pan. Shake every so often. Sprinkle with flour, add cream and a dash of liquid if it's all a bit too thick. Stir in almonds. Can be used as a supplementary vegetable or served in a border of duchesse potato to make a main course in its own right.

Courgettes à la Polonaise

1½ lb. courgettes
4 oz. butter
1 heaped tbs. flour
½ pint milk
juice of ½ lemon
4 oz. breadcrumbs

4–6 hardboiled eggs
1 tbs. chopped parsley
1 tsp. grated lemon rind
salt and pepper
lemon slices and fresh
    parsley to garnish

Wash, top and tail and slice courgettes into ¼″ slices. Sauté in a quarter of the butter, turning frequently, until tender. Meanwhile use another quarter of the butter to make a sauce, melting butter, then adding flour, cooking for a minute or two, then removing from heat and gradually adding milk. Return to heat to thicken, carefully add lemon juice and seasoning, then simmer gently over a low heat while preparing the polonaise topping. To do this, fry the breadcrumbs in the rest of the butter until golden and crisp. Finely chop hardboiled eggs and add to the breadcrumbs with the parsley, lemon rind and salt and pepper to taste.

To assemble, put courgettes on warm serving dish; pour the sauce over and top with the breadcrumb mixture. Garnish with lemon slices and fresh parsley.

Many other vegetables are delicious served in this way. Make *leek, onion, mushrooms* or *spinach à la polonaise* in exactly the same way. *Aubergines and peppers à la polonaise* are very good; salt aubergines first, then sauté with some chopped peppers, onions and perhaps tomatoes and mushrooms, as for courgettes à la polonaise. Some vegetables, such as *cauliflower, celery, jerusalem artichokes* and *fennel* need to be cooked first in a little water, before being tossed in the melted butter. For a really economical dish, try using carrots and cabbage. In any case, allow $1\frac{1}{2}$–2 lbs. of vegetables.

Courgettes Mornay

$1\frac{1}{2}$–2 lbs. courgettes	3 oz. grated cheese
1 bayleaf	salt and pepper
2 oz. butter	2 oz. fresh breadcrumbs
2 heaped tbs. flour	a little extra grated cheese
$\frac{3}{4}$ pint milk	and pieces of butter to top
$\frac{1}{4}$ pint white wine	

Wash courgettes; cut off stalks and cut courgettes into $\frac{1}{2}''$ pieces. Cook in a little fast boiling water with bayleaf, until tender, then drain well and keep warm. Make a good cheese sauce by melting butter, adding the flour, and when it froths, drawing pan off heat and adding milk. Return to heat and thicken, stirring all the time, then carefully stir in the wine, a little at a time. Simmer gently for a minute or two longer, then draw off heat, add grated cheese and seasoning. Put courgettes in a shallow ovenproof dish, pour sauce over and top with breadcrumbs, grated cheese and some little pieces of butter. Place under a moderate grill or in the oven for about 15 minutes, until golden and bubbly.

For a slightly different presentation, use a large, shallow ovenproof dish; place the courgettes and sauce in the middle and cover with the topping, as above. Then pipe around the outside with creamy mashed potato, using a large shell nozzle. Place under grill to crisp the topping and lightly brown the potato, and serve garnished with parsley, tomato slices, lemon slices or what-you-will.

This simple way of preparing vegetables is also one of the nicest, with the contrast between the texture of rich creamy sauce, the vegetables, which should be tender but firm, and the crispy topping. Many other vegetables can be used – good old *cauliflower*, of course, also *celery* or *fennel* (all of which benefit from the addition of a few button mushrooms, sautéed in butter); or for a no-expense-spared occasion, try *asparagus*, which is best first steamed (or use the canned variety – 2 or even 3 large cans, and drain well). *Canned sweetcorn* is also good – use 2 cans. *Jerusalem artichokes* and *salsify* can both be used. Put the peeled vegetables straight into cold water (don't worry too much about the lumpy bits when peeling the artichokes) to which a little vinegar has been added to prevent discolouration. *Vegetable marrow, baby onions* and *leeks* are all good candidates for this dish, but these three are best sautéed until tender, rather than cooked in boiling water. So, sauté them, then drain off excess liquid, and proceed as above. A lovely mixture can be made from *aubergines, peppers, onions and mushrooms* – make up 2 lbs. of vegetables altogether, then slice them and sauté them until tender, drain off liquid for use in soups or sauces and proceed as above.

Courgettes au Parmesan

8 courgettes	salt and pepper
butter	grated parmesan cheese
1 finely chopped clove garlic	2 tsp. protoveg smoky
finely chopped parsley	snaps

Cut the courgettes in half lengthwise. Dot each face with butter, garlic and parsley, salt and pepper, a layer of cheese and a scattering of smoky snaps. Grill for a couple of minutes or so. The top should cook, while the courgettes stay crisp and half-raw. Serve with creamed potatoes and tomato sauce, p. 157.

Creamy Cucumber and Mushrooms

4 oz. almonds	salt, pepper and nutmeg
1 large cucumber	to serve:
$\frac{1}{2}$ lb. button mushrooms	cooked rice, or creamy
3 sprigs mint	mashed potato
3 tbs. vegetable oil	lemon slices
squeeze lemon juice	omelette strips, made from
$\frac{1}{2}$ lb. cream cheese	2 eggs, p. 111

Skin almonds by putting into small pan of cold water, boiling for 2 minutes, draining and rubbing off skins. Cut into shreds. Peel and dice cucumber; wash and slice mushrooms. Sauté almonds, cucumber, mushrooms and mint in the oil for 5 minutes. Add lemon juice, cream cheese and seasoning. Heat through and serve in a border of cooked rice or creamy mashed potato. Garnish with lemon slices and a lattice of omelette strips.

Other combinations are delicious. *Creamy courgettes and mushrooms* are made in exactly the same way, using $1\frac{1}{2}$ lb. courgettes instead of the cucumber. Try *artichoke hearts and mushrooms*, replacing cucumber with 2 cans drained artichoke hearts. Or what about *creamy asparagus and mushrooms*, made by using 2 cans of asparagus instead of cucumber, or *creamy celery and mushrooms* in which cucumber is replaced by one very large can of celery hearts, or 2 or 3 nice fresh celery hearts, sliced and steamed, or boiled in a very little water until tender.

Mixed Vegetable Chop Suey

1 lb. white cabbage	1 tbs. soy sauce
2 onions	2 tsp. cornflour
1 green pepper	$\frac{3}{4}$ pint cold water
2 cloves garlic	2 tbs. oil
1 piece stem ginger	1 can bean sprouts
(optional)	6 oz. blanched almonds
$\frac{1}{2}$ lb. button mushrooms	salt, pepper and sugar
2 sticks celery	boiled rice to serve

Shred cabbage finely; chop onions and green pepper, crush garlic and ginger; slice mushrooms and celery thinly. It gives a more oriental look if celery is sliced at an angle rather than straight across. Mix together soy sauce, cornflour and water. This preparation can all be done in advance. Ten minutes before the meal heat the oil in a wide saucepan and toss in prepared vegetables. Stir over a high heat for 3 minutes – do not brown. Add cornflour solution, bean sprouts and almonds and stir until mixture thickens, then cover and simmer for 3 minutes. Season carefully with salt, pepper and sugar. Pour into centre of hot serving dish and surround with cooked rice. Serve with soy sauce.

Variations

Mixed Vegetable Chop Suey with Egg

Egg can be used to provide the protein in this dish, replacing some or all of the blanched almonds. Just before serving make two 2-egg omelettes, cut omelettes into slices and arrange criss-cross fashion on top of chop suey, or mix in lightly with the vegetables, or use hard-boiled eggs, sliced and arranged round dish.

I love this Chinese way of preparing food: it is clean, quick, and very tasty and of course, many other vegetables can be treated in this way. I have often used it for purely English vegetables, such as cabbage, carrots and onions, garnished with egg strips to produce a cheap meal in under 15 minutes! Any combination of vegetable you happen to have to hand can be used: just see there is a bottle of soy sauce and if possible a jar of preserved stem ginger in the house, and you're well away.

Carrot and Cabbage Chop Suey

Try this for an economy 'meal-out-of-nothing' version! Follow above, but omit such luxuries as mushrooms, green pepper and bean sprouts, and use instead 1 lb. carrots with the cabbage. Cut carrots thinly slantwise for a Chinese look. If no blanched almonds are available, use the egg variation (see above). Season carefully with salt, pepper and sugar. Can also be served with grated cheese or hardboiled eggs replacing the almonds for protein. *Cauliflower and carrot chop suey* is another economy variation, or, for late summer days, I often make *runner bean chop suey* – sounds terribly English, doesn't it, but the runner beans mix in very well with the cabbage and carrot variation – I cut the beans diagonally to give a Chinese look to the dish. Also for the late summer, *vegetable marrow chop suey* is very quick and easy – make the cabbage and carrot variation, but use vegetable marrow instead of some of the cabbage and carrot.

Mixed Vegetable Curry

1 lb. potatoes
1 lb. leeks
1 small cauliflower
4 oz. pkt. frozen peas

sauce:
1 clove garlic
1 onion
4 tbs. oil
2½ tsp. ground coriander

2½ tsp. ground cumin
½ tsp. curry powder
½ tsp. turmeric
½ tsp. white mustard seed
1 bayleaf
8 oz. can tomatoes
¾ pint water
1 tsp. garam masala
salt and pepper
4–6 hardboiled eggs or roasted almonds or cashew-nuts to serve

Peel and cube potatoes; cook in boiling water until just tender. Just before potatoes are cooked add leeks cut into 1″ pieces, and cauliflower in florets; finally add peas. Meanwhile make the sauce; crush garlic, chop onion and sauté in oil until onion is soft and lightly browned, then add all the spices and bayleaf and cook for about 2 minutes. Add tomatoes and water and simmer gently for 10–15 minutes to allow flavours to blend. Add garam masala and salt and pepper, then add drained, cooked vegetables and allow to heat thoroughly in the sauce. Serve with cooked rice and hardboiled eggs or roasted nuts for protein, also any trimmings desired: mango chutney, lime pickle and poppadoms.

Other combinations of vegetables can of course be used; the potatoes can be replaced by aubergines or marrow and the leeks with canned okra.

Mixed Vegetable Platter

1 lb. courgettes	1–2 oz. butter
$\frac{1}{2}$ lb. french beans	6 hardboiled eggs
$\frac{1}{2}$ lb. small carrots	juice of $\frac{1}{2}$ lemon
$\frac{1}{2}$ lb. button onions	fresh parsley sprigs
$\frac{1}{2}$ lb. frozen sweetcorn	1 pint lemon sauce or
6 tomatoes	hollandaise sauce or
$\frac{1}{2}$ lb. button mushrooms	green herb sauce

Wash and top and tail courgettes and beans (or use frozen beans); scrape carrots, leave whole; peel onions. Cook vegetables in separate pans in a little boiling water until tender. Cook sweetcorn according to directions on packet. Halve tomatoes widthwise; scoop out pulp, and chop. Wash and chop mushrooms and sauté gently in one-third of the butter with the tomato pulp for 5 minutes, then heap into tomato halves. Place under a moderate grill for 5–10 minutes to cook tomatoes. Slice eggs and keep warm. When ready to serve, arrange the vegetables attractively on a large warmed plate. Melt rest of butter, mix with lemon juice and pour over vegetables. Garnish each tomato half with a parsley sprig. Serve with the sauce of your choice – lemon sauce or hollandaise sauce or one of the others given in the sauce section, starting on p. 152. Many other combinations of vegetables can of course be used, aiming for as gay and varied a mixture as possible. Aubergines, sliced, salted, drained and then fried are good, also peppers, sliced and lightly fried; small new potatoes, steamed or boiled, are also nice included in this. Also, any of the stuffed vegetables in the section starting on p. 125, can form the centrepiece and source of protein for the Mixed Vegetable Platter; hardboiled eggs can then be omitted and the whole dish served with a suitable sauce.

Variations

Mixed Vegetable Platter Duchesse

Using a large shell nozzle pipe a border of duchesse potatoes around a large, shallow ovenproof dish; brown in a moderate oven, 350 °F., gas mark 4, or under a moderate grill, for 20–30 minutes, then arrange vegetables as above.

Mixed Vegetable Platter with Croûtons

The hardboiled eggs can be omitted, and the dish garnished with crispy almond slices, p. 82.

Mixed Vegetable Platter with Egg Sauce

Omit hardboiled eggs from recipe, and serve with egg sauce, p. 153.

Mixed Vegetable Platter Mornay

Omit eggs from recipe. Scatter top of vegetables generously with toasted flaked almonds, and serve with cheese sauce, p. 153.

Mixed Winter Vegetable Platter with Dhal Sauce

1 lb. leeks	1 oz. melted butter
¾ lb. carrots	chopped parsley
1 small cauliflower	1 pint dhal sauce
4 tomatoes	lemon slices to garnish

This might be called an economy version of Mixed Vegetable Platter! It is also good for winter. Slit leeks and wash; cut into 1″ pieces. Scrape carrots and cut into matchsticks; wash cauliflower and break into florets. Cook vegetables separately until tender; drain. Halve tomatoes; grill for 5–10 minutes. Arrange vegetables on a hot serving dish; pour over melted butter; scatter with chopped parsley, garnish with nice chunky lemon slices, and serve with dhal sauce, which is very easy to make, see p. 155, and provides the protein for this meal. Of course other sauces could be used: mornay sauce, for instance, with plenty of cheese in it for protein; or egg sauce – or hardboiled eggs could be included in the platter and the whole served with parsley or lemon sauce.

Potato Pizza

2 large onions	1 lb. potatoes
vegetable oil	salt and pepper
½ lb. tomatoes	6 oz. grated cheese
6 oz. mushrooms	

This is a quick family dish. Peel and slice onions and sauté in a little oil until tender, then add the tomatoes, peeled and sliced and the mushrooms, sliced but not peeled and cook until mushrooms are tender. Meanwhile, peel and coarsely grate potatoes; heat a little oil in a frying pan and press potatoes into this; press down firmly and fry with a lid on the pan until bottom of potato round is golden brown and crispy, then carefully turn over, using a fish slice, and fry second side until golden brown. Arrange onions, tomatoes and mushrooms on top, sprinkled generously with the cheese and place under a moderate grill until cheese is golden and bubbly.

Ratatouille

2 large aubergines	1 lb. vegetable marrow,
salt	courgettes or
1 clove garlic, crushed	cucumber
2 large onions	6 tbs. oil
2 green or red peppers	pepper and sugar
4 large tomatoes, peeled	2 tbs. chopped parsley
	grated cheese

Cube aubergines (do not peel); sprinkle with salt, leave for 30 minutes, then squeeze out and discard juice. Crush garlic, peel and slice onions, peppers, tomatoes and marrow, courgettes or cucumber. Heat oil and add vegetables, stir well, clap lid on pan and cook over a very low heat for 30 minutes, or until all vegetables are tender. Season with salt, pepper and sugar. Serve sprinkled with chopped parsley and surrounded with plenty of grated cheese. When marrows are cheap and good, I often use more marrow and omit aubergines from recipe. It's well worth while making plenty of this; cold, it makes an excellent salad. Very good with crusty bread. It also makes a lovely starter to a meal, served either hot or cold.

VEGETARIAN PROTEIN FOODS

At the time of writing much research is going into the manufacture of new forms of protein made from simple, cheap vegetable sources. Two such foods already available are protoveg, a textured protein made from soya, and marigold vegetarian meat. These foods are highly nutritious, being superior in food value, ounce for ounce, to best beef, at a fraction of the price. They come in dehydrated pieces (looking rather like dog biscuits – don't be put off!), store well and are easily and quickly prepared in a little water or stock in anything from 5 to 30 minutes or more – the time varies according to the size of the chunks. The large chunks benefit greatly from 2 hours' soaking and long, slow cooking until tender. Herbs, spices and flavourings can be added to the water or some or all of the water can be replaced by wine. These vegetarian protein foods open up new possibilities for the creative cook. We have enjoyed the following recipes which can be made with either protoveg or marigold vegetarian meat, or, if preferred, with canned vegetarian foods such as nuttolene, meatless steaks and tartex savoury roll which are established favourites with many vegetarians, and imaginatively used in savoury dishes can prove attractive to meat-eaters too.

Vegetarian Chicken Pieces à la Ritz

can of sliced chicken-flavour soya protein	$\frac{1}{2}$ red pepper glass of sherry
2 tbs. vegetable oil	small carton of
4 oz. mushrooms	double cream
$\frac{1}{2}$ green pepper	salt and pepper

Wash the soya chicken slices and break up into pieces. Fry sliced mushrooms, finely chopped green and red peppers, then add chicken pieces, a glass of sherry and the cream. Simmer very gently so that the chicken pieces absorb the flavours but don't disintegrate. Season, and serve with grilled tomatoes and french beans.

Fricassé Forestière

5 oz. pkt. chunky
unflavoured protoveg or
marigold vegetarian meat
½ pint white wine or white
stock
1 bayleaf
1 large clove garlic
1 oz. butter

1 tbs. oil
1 tsp. lemon juice
1 heaped tsp. flour
½ pint single cream or
top milk
½ lb. button mushrooms,
sliced
salt and pepper

Hydrate the protoveg or marigold vegetarian meat by
soaking in the liquid for 1 hour or so; then simmer with
bayleaf for 30 minutes, adding more liquid if necessary.
Drain and sauté with the crushed or finely chopped garlic
in the oil and half the butter for 2 or 3 minutes. Sprinkle
with the lemon juice, salt and pepper, and leave on one
side while making the sauce. To make the sauce, melt
rest of butter in a clean pan, add the flour, stir for 1
minute, but do not brown, then add the cream and thinly
slice button mushrooms (ordinary flat mushrooms are
unsuitable as they discolour the sauce). Cook very gently
for 10 minutes, season carefully, then add the protein
mixture, heat through; serve immediately.

Fricassé Béchamel

2½ oz. protoveg or mari-
gold vegetarian meat
½ pint white wine or
stock
½ pint milk
1 bayleaf
piece pared lemon rind

1 oz. butter or margarine
1 large onion
1 oz. flour
grating of nutmeg
1 tbs. lemon juice
salt and pepper
lemon wedges to garnish
parsley

Soak and simmer protoveg or vitpro as in previous
recipe. Meanwhile bring milk, bayleaf and lemon rind
to the boil and then remove from heat and leave to infuse
for 15 minutes. Melt butter in a pan and lightly fry finely

chopped onion until soft but not browned. Stir in flour, cook for 2 minutes, then strain in milk. Allow to thicken over heat, stirring all the time, then simmer gently for 5 minutes. Stir in cooked protoveg or marigold vegetarian meat, season with nutmeg, lemon juice, salt and pepper, and continue to simmer very gently until ready to serve garnished with lemon wedges, and parsley if available.

Fritters

3 oz. flavoured chunky
  protoveg or marigold
  vegetarian meat
just under ½ pint water
  or red wine
1 bayleaf
vegetable oil

1 large onion
4 oz. flour
½ tsp. mixed herbs
1 egg
salt and pepper
6 fl. oz. milk and water
  mixed

Soak and simmer protoveg or marigold vegetarian meat as for Fricassé Forestière, p. 146. Meanwhile heat a little oil in a frying pan and fry the finely chopped onion until lightly browned. Sift the flour into a bowl, make a well in the centre and add the egg, beat well and gradually beat in the milk. Season with salt, pepper and the mixed herbs. Stir in the cooked protein food. Heat some more oil in the pan and drop in spoonfuls of the mixture, frying until crisp and brown and turning them over. Serve with creamed potatoes and brown sauce.

Goulash – Vegetarian Style

5 oz. chunky beef flavoured
  protoveg or marigold
  vegetarian meat
½ pint red wine
2 bayleaves
2 large cloves garlic
3 oz. butter
1 tbs. oil

4 onions
8 oz. can pimentos
10 oz. can tomatoes
½ tsp. paprika
salt and pepper
2 tbs. tomato purée
freshly chopped parsley

Soak and simmer the protoveg or vitpro as for Fricassé Forestière, p. 146. Drain off and reserve any liquid left in pan. Crush garlic and add to protoveg or vitpro, mixing well. Melt two-thirds of the butter and half the oil in a large frying pan and sauté the protein food in this until golden and crisp all over. Remove from pan and keep hot. Slice onions in rings and fry lightly in the remaining butter and oil until tender but not brown. Add pimentos and tomatoes, together with their liquid and the reserved liquid which the protein was cooked in, also the tomato purée. Season with salt, pepper and paprika. Heat through thoroughly, then add the hot protein food, mix well, check seasoning and serve with plain boiled rice or creamed potatoes.

Mixed Grill

5 oz. chunky flavoured protoveg or marigold vegetarian meat	a pinch each of mace, salt, pepper and paprika
$\frac{3}{4}$ pint water or red wine	2 oz. butter
2 bayleaves	2 tbs. oil
2 large cloves garlic	4 large onions, sliced
2 heaped tbs. flour	4 large tomatoes
$\frac{1}{2}$ tsp. dry mustard	8 oz. mushrooms

Soak and simmer protoveg or vitpro as for Fricassé Forestière, p. 146, drain. Crush garlic, add to protoveg or vitpro, mixing well. Mix together flour, dry mustard, mace, salt and pepper, paprika, and toss protein food in this to coat evenly. Melt butter and oil in frying pan and sauté protoveg or marigold vegetarian meat until golden brown and crisp all over. It will probably be necessary to fry it in two or more batches, depending on the size of the frying pan. Meanwhile, slice onions, brush with oil and place under moderate grill, turning frequently. When nearly tender (about 10 minutes) add tomatoes and mushrooms to grill pan, brush with oil and grill for about

10 minutes until all are cooked. Serve with the protoveg or vitpro and a good savoury sauce.

Quick Mushroom Savoury

1 large onion	10 oz. can nuttolene
1 oz. butter	1 tbs. vegetarian gravy powder
6 oz. mushrooms	$\frac{1}{3}$ pint water

A family quickie, popular with children: chop onion and fry in the butter for 5 minutes; add the washed and sliced mushrooms and fry for a further 4–5 minutes. Dice nuttolene and add to mushroom mixture; then sprinkle the gravy powder over and mix well; gradually add the water and simmer until thickened.

Serve hot with creamed potatoes, carrots and a cooked green vegetable.

Stroganoff – Vegetarian Style

5 oz. chunky flavoured protoveg or marigold vegetarian meat	1 tbs. oil
	1 small onion
1 bayleaf	$\frac{1}{2}$ lb. button mushrooms
$\frac{3}{4}$ pint water or red wine	$\frac{1}{4}$ pint sour cream
1 clove garlic	salt and pepper
1 oz. butter	pinch mace or grated nutmeg

Soak and simmer protoveg or vitpro as for Fricassé Forestière, p. 146. Strain off and reserve any liquid. Crush garlic and fry with the protoveg or marigold vegetarian meat in the butter and oil until golden and crisp. Add the onion and fry until soft, then add sliced button mushrooms and cook until tender. Add sour cream and salt, pepper and mace or nutmeg to taste. Allow cream to heat through (but not boil) then serve. I like to garnish this with croûtons of fried bread.

Nuttolene with Lemon Mayonnaise Sauce

1 large can nuttolene or tartex savoury roll or 13 oz. can chicken flavoured soya protein, drained and rinsed.	½ pint quick mayonnaise, p. 73 crumbs for topping

Arrange thin slices nuttolene, savoury roll or soya protein in a shallow casserole, with a good dollop of the mayonnaise between each layer, ending with mayonnaise. Leave to marinade for at least 30 minutes – 2 hours or more if possible. Sprinkle with breadcrumbs and bake in a moderate oven for 20 minutes.

Paupiettes of Meatless Steak

1 medium onion, chopped	1 tbs. fresh breadcrumbs
4 oz. mushrooms	1 tbs chopped parsley
1 tbs. protoveg smoky snaps	salt, pepper, thyme
½ oz. butter	beaten egg
1 tbs. oil	large can meatless steaks
1 tbs. finely chopped lemon peel	flour to coat
	red wine or water
	clove garlic, crushed
	a little mustard

Fry the onion, mushrooms and smoky snaps in the butter and oil. Add the lemon peel, breadcrumbs, parsley, seasoning and beaten egg. Slit each steak lengthways (not quite cutting it in half) to form a pocket, and insert some of the mushroom stuffing mixture. Coat in flour and sauté these steaks on a medium flame in a little oil. Add liquid just to cover, plus any remaining mushroom mixture, and simmer gently for about 15 minutes. They can be prepared early and reheated. To serve, lay the paupiettes on a dish, add garlic and mustard to remaining sauce and heat fiercely for a minute or two before pouring on top of paupiettes. Serve with a bland potato dish (baked, maybe, or creamed) and some nice buttered french beans.

Textured Vegetable Protein Curry

3 medium onions
2 cloves garlic
1½ tbs. vegetable oil
2 full tsp. mild curry powder
½ tsp. ginger

small can tomato purée
2 medium potatoes
1 cup of reconstituted protoveg or marigold vegetarian meat
¾ pint water
salt and pepper

Fry sliced onions and garlic in oil on medium heat, browning slightly but keeping soft. Add a dessertspoon of water if needed. Add curry powder and ginger, turn heat down, stir for a couple of minutes, then add tomato purée, the potatoes, peeled and cut small, and the hydrated protoveg or marigold vegetarian meat and stir for another 2 minutes – add another spoon of water if needed, then add ¾ pint water and cook for about ½ hour until the protein is tender. Season with salt and pepper to taste, and serve with fried rice, p. 114, or plain boiled rice.

Vegetarian Pork Chunks in Ginger Cream Sauce

small carton sour cream
1 tbs. tomato paste
finely chopped clove garlic
a little mustard
2–3 tbs. dill pickle
1 tsp. grated fresh ginger or 1½ tsp. ground ginger

pinch rosemary, marjoram, oregano, caraway seed, salt, pepper
1 cup protoveg pork chunks
about 6 spring onions
1 oz. butter
flour
orange segments to decorate

Mix together the sour cream, tomato paste, finely chopped clove of garlic, mustard, dill pickle, ginger and seasonings. Sauté the spring onions, stalks and bulbs, in half the butter, add a little flour to take up excess fat, and enough water to make a thickish sauce, then add the cream mixture. Hydrate the pork chunks as directed and fry in the rest of the butter, then lay them in a serving dish, pour the cooked sauce over them, and maybe crisp under the grill. Decorate with orange slices.

SAUCES

Unlike the majority of recipes in this book, those for sauces are not calculated for 100 per cent wholemeal flour, but for 81 per cent which is better for this particular purpose as it is more glutinous. Cornflour could be used, though I prefer the more natural wholemeal flour, albeit 81 per cent. If using cornflour, use half the quantity given for flour.

It is very helpful to make up a good quantity of sauce béchamel and keep it ready in the fridge. It can be gently reheated, preferably but not essentially in a double saucepan, and a good beating with a whisk will make it smooth – actually in all saucemaking a whisk is a better friend than a wooden spoon when it comes to adding the liquid.

Sauce Béchamel

2 oz. butter	1 bayleaf
2 heaped tbs. flour	salt and pepper
1 pint milk	

Melt butter; add flour and cook gently until it froths. Remove from heat and gradually add milk, stirring all the time. Add bayleaf, return to heat and stir until thickened. Season, and simmer for 15 minutes.

Variations

Asparagus Sauce

Add ½ can chopped asparagus and a little lemon juice to basic sauce béchamel. Asparagus liquid can be made up to 1 pint with milk and used to make sauce.

Sauce Aurore

Add 2–3 tbs. tomato purée and a touch of sugar and lemon juice to sauce béchamel.

Celery Sauce

3–4 tbs. very finely chopped celery and ½ tsp. celery salt can be added to sauce after milk and simmered in it until tender.

Cheese Sauce

Make sauce béchamel. Draw off heat after sauce has simmered and add 3–4 oz. grated cheese and a pinch of dried mustard or cayenne pepper.

Egg Sauce

Made by adding 3 hardboiled eggs, very finely chopped, to basic sauce béchamel.

Fennel Sauce

Add to the sauce 2–3 tbs. very finely chopped fennel bulb (that is, the vegetable, not the herb). Add with the milk and simmer until fennel is cooked.

Green Herb Sauce

Use any fresh green herbs available, 1–2 tbs. very finely chopped, and added just before serving.

Sauce Tartare

Add ¼ pint mayonnaise – homemade mayonnaise is best – or Hellmans bottled mayonnaise – and 1 tbs.

lemon juice to sauce béchamel, also 1–2 tbs. chopped gherkins and 1 tbs. capers.

Mushroom Sauce

Wash and finely slice 8–10 button mushrooms and add to sauce béchamel. Simmer for 5–10 minutes to cook mushrooms.

Mustard Sauce

Add 1 tbs. french mustard to sauce béchamel.

Onion Sauce

Finely chop 1 large onion and sauté in the butter until tender. Then add flour and proceed as for sauce béchamel.

Parsley Sauce

2 tbs. parsley, finely chopped, added to sauce béchamel.

Sauce Piquante

Add 1 tbs. chopped red peppers, 1 tbs. onion, 1 tbs. cider vinegar, 1 tbs. chopped gherkins to sauce béchamel.

Curry Sauce – English

1 onion	2 tbs. flour
1 apple	1 pint water
1 tbs. curry powder	1 tbs. tomato purée
2 tbs. oil	salt, pepper and lemon juice

Chop onion and apple and fry with curry powder in the oil until tender. Stir in flour, cook for 2 minutes and then remove from heat and add water, tomato purée, salt, pepper and lemon juice. Simmer for 15 minutes.

Curry Sauce – Indian

4 tbs. oil	$\frac{1}{2}$ tsp. white mustard seed
1 clove garlic	1 bayleaf
1 onion	8 oz. can tomatoes
$2\frac{1}{2}$ tsp. ground coriander	$\frac{3}{4}$ pint water
$2\frac{1}{2}$ tsp. ground cumin	1 tsp. garam masala
$\frac{1}{2}$ tsp. curry powder	salt and pepper
$\frac{1}{2}$ tsp. turmeric	

Heat oil in pan and add crushed garlic and peeled and chopped onion. Fry gently until onion is soft and lightly browned, then add all the spices and the bayleaf, cook for 2 minutes longer, then add the tomatoes and water and simmer gently for 10–15 minutes for flavours to mellow and blend. Add garam masala and salt and pepper just before serving. Sauce can be liquidised or strained if desired.

This sauce is not 'hot' but is full of flavour. Spices can usually be obtained from health stores, delicatessens or supermarkets, otherwise from the address on page 194.

Dhal Sauce

4 oz. lentils	2 tsp. curry powder
1 pint water	juice and rind of 1 lemon
1 onion	salt and pepper
1 tbs. oil	

Soak lentils overnight in water. Next day simmer until tender. Meanwhile chop onion and sauté gently in the oil with the curry powder for 10 minutes. Add juice and grated rind of lemon and then liquidise. Season well with salt and pepper.

Sauce Espagnole – Brown Sauce

1 tbs. oil	1 bayleaf
1 onion, peeled	1 tsp. yeast extract
1 clove garlic, peeled	2 tbs. tomato purée (optional)
2 tbs. flour	salt and pepper
$1\frac{1}{2}$ pints water	1 tbs. sherry (optional)

Heat oil and fry chopped onion and garlic until lightly browned. Add flour and stir until browned, then add water, bayleaf and yeast extract, and simmer for 10–15 minutes. Strain; add tomato purée, if using, and salt and pepper to taste.

For special occasions, if liked, 1 tbs. sherry may be added before serving.

Sauce Hollandaise

1 tsp. lemon juice 2 egg yolks
1 tbs. cold water   4 oz. butter
salt and pepper

Mix together lemon juice, water, salt and pepper in top of double saucepan or a bowl set over a pan of hot water – water must not boil. Beat in egg yolks then whisk in a quarter of the butter, beating until butter has melted and sauce is beginning to thicken. Then add the rest of the butter in three batches; beat well. Add a little more lemon juice if liked to taste.

Lemon Sauce

juice and rind of 1 lemon 1 pint milk
2 oz. butter   salt, pepper and sugar
2 heaped tbs. flour

Thinly pare lemon rind; snip into shreds. Melt butter and add flour; when it froths remove from heat and add milk. Return to heat and simmer for 10 minutes, then add lemon juice and rind. Season with salt, pepper and sugar.

Orange Sauce

Make as for Lemon Sauce, using 1 orange instead of 1 lemon.

Sweet Sour Sauce

1 onion	1 tsp. sugar
1 tbs. oil	1 tsp. soy sauce
2 tsp. cornflour	8 oz. can pineapple
¾ pint water	½ very small green pepper
¼ tsp. dry mustard	1 tomato, skinned
1 tbs. cider vinegar	salt and pepper

Finely chop onion and fry gently in the oil. When tender add cornflour. Remove from heat, add water stirring all the time. Simmer gently for 5 minutes. Add mustard, cider vinegar, sugar, soy sauce, chopped and drained canned pineapple, chopped green pepper and tomato. Season well with salt and pepper and simmer for 2–3 minutes longer.

Tomato Sauce

1 small onion	1 pint water
1 clove garlic	2 tbs. tomato purée
2 oz. butter	salt, sugar and pepper
2 heaped tbs. flour	

Finely chop onion, crush garlic. Fry gently in the butter until tender. Add flour; when it froths remove from heat and add water and tomato purée. Return to heat stirring until thickened. Season with salt, sugar and pepper, and simmer for 15 minutes.

Wine Sauce

1½ oz. butter	½ pint stock
8 button mushrooms	wineglass of red wine
3 tomatoes, skinned	1 tsp. brown sugar
¼ tsp. mixed herbs	salt and pepper to taste
1 heaped tbs. flour	

Melt the butter in a saucepan and add the chopped mushrooms and tomatoes and herbs and cook for 5–10 minutes. Add the flour and stir for 2 minutes, then remove from heat and gradually add the stock. Return to the heat and simmer for 5 minutes. Add the wine and season to taste with sugar, salt and pepper. Sauce can be thinned down with a little more stock if necessary.

V

DESSERTS, GATEAUX, BISCUITS AND BREADS

Since gorgeous gateaux make splendid desserts, I've put them together in one chapter, which contains desserts for all occasions – healthy figure-wise desserts such as fresh fruit compôtes and yoghurts, and the more elaborate something-special-and-never-mind-the-calories type.

While cakes and biscuits and gateaux certainly have their place in life, I do think they should know that place and not be allowed to play too big a part! Natural sugar, in the form of fresh and dried fruit is far better – for our figures and the children's teeth, as well as their future, if not present figures.

CREAMS, ICECREAMS AND YOGHURT
Special Chocolate Icecream

4 oz. plain chocolate	1 tsp. instant coffee dissolved
½ pint single cream	in 1 tbs. boiling water
½ pint double cream	1 tbs. clear honey

Break up the chocolate and melt in a bowl set over a pan of gently steaming water. Meanwhile whip creams together. Add coffee dissolved in the water, honey and melted chocolate. Turn into a polythene container and freeze until set. Serve with fan wafers.

Chocolate Icecream Christmas Pudding

Make the icecream as above and while the mixture is freezing cover the following with sweet sherry:

4 tbs. glacé cherries
2 tbs. flaked almonds
2 tbs. chopped angelica

2 tbs. chopped glacé
pineapple
2 tbs. sultanas

Leave to soak overnight if possible. Next day beat into the frozen icecream and smooth into a foil-lined pudding basin; refreeze. To serve: turn out on a plate topped with whipped cream and push a foil-protected piece of holly into the top.

Pineapple Cream

1 large pineapple or a large
can (1 lb. 13½ oz.)
pineapple pieces
2 tbs. icing sugar if using
fresh pineapple

½ pint double cream
1–2 tbs. grand marnier
(optional)
To decorate:
crystallised roses and
violets, fresh green
bayleaves if
available

If using fresh pineapple, remove skin and hard core and dice flesh, sprinkle with icing sugar. If using canned, drain off syrup. Whip cream stiffly; add liqueur if using and whip again lightly, then fold in pineapple. Serve piled up on a dish – preferably a stem glass cakedish. Stud with crystallised roses and violets to give a jewelled effect, and if possible tuck fresh green bayleaves point outwards, around base. Serve with sponge finger biscuits or shortbreads.

Prune Cream

1 lb. prunes
sweet white wine
½ pint double cream

1 tsp. grated orange rind
sugar or honey to taste
orange slices to decorate

Soak prunes overnight in water or sweet white wine. Next day simmer gently until soft. Stone and sieve or liquidise with enough of their liquid to make a thick purée. Cool. Whip cream and fold in prune purée and orange rind and sugar or honey if required, to taste. Serve chilled; garnish with orange slices.

Ratafia Cream

8 oz. ratafias	2 tbs. sweet white wine
½ pint double cream	½ oz. sugar
½ pint single cream	2 oz. toasted almonds

Crush ratafias. Whip creams, fold in wine, sugar and ratafias. Spoon into individual glasses to serve and sprinkle generously with toasted almonds.

Zabaglione

4 large egg yolks	3 tbs. sweet white wine
1 oz. caster sugar	1 tbs. marsala

Put egg yolks and sugar in a bowl. Whisk together over hot water until thick and light, then add the white wine and a little marsala to taste. Pour into glasses, and serve warm, with sponge fingers.

A good economy version of this can be made without the marsala, or for those who do not like wine it could be made using 4 tbs. grape juice.

Yoghurt

Yoghurt is one of the simplest and most nourishing foods available. Rich in calcium and protein and supplying during the process of digestion valuable B vitamins, it has often been called a wonder food.

Apart from its food value real yoghurt is useful for nervous indigestion and stomach complaints, and after treatment with antibiotics, being light and easily assimilated, yet extremely nourishing. The vital calcium it supplies is useful in any diet, but particularly in the diets of those who are highly strung.

Homemade Yoghurt

1 pint longlife (UHT) milk
1 desstsp. live bulgarian yoghurt

The easiest way of making yoghurt is to use a home
yoghurt maker such as the 'Yoghurtera' which will keep
a jar containing the milk and 'starter' yoghurt at just the
right temperature for making the yoghurt. If one of these
is available, simply put the 'starter' yoghurt into the jar,
stir in the cold UHT milk, place jar in the yoghurt
maker, replace cover and leave for about 8 hours until
yoghurt is firm. Keep in fridge and use as required.

If a yoghurt maker is not available you need one or
two large jars and a warm place such as an airing cupboard. Warm jars, heat UHT milk to blood heat, divide
yoghurt 'starter' between jars and pour in the warm
milk, stirring until smooth. Place jars in a suitable warm
place and leave for about 5–8 hours depending on the
degree of warmth, until firm.

Before I had a yoghurt maker I used to have success-
ful results by wrapping the warm jars in an old warmed
blanket and placing on a warm mantelpiece. Once you
have found a suitable warm place, yoghurt is easily and
quickly made at home. Reserve a dessertspoonful of
yoghurt each time to start off a new batch.

Vegan Yoghurt

Is made in exactly the same way, only using plantmilk
instead of dairy milk.

Yoghurt Pots

1 pint longlife (UHT) milk
1 desstsp. live bulgarian yoghurt

Use individual ramekins for this, or little earthenware
yoghurt pots. Warm the pots. Heat milk to blood tem-

perature, add yoghurt and mix very thoroughly. Pour into the warmed pots, put in a warm place, such as an airing cupboard or by a radiator. I use the warm mantelpiece above our coalfire, but if you do this be prepared for an influx of visitors, for they inevitably 'drop in' when the sitting-room looks like a miniature yoghurt factory! Anyway, leave them in their warm place until the milk turns to firm yoghurt, this takes anything from 4–8 hours, then put them into the fridge. Serve chilled with a topping of demerara sugar (which can be sprinkled on top, then caramelised under the grill) or some chopped dried fruit, or a canned apricot and some sieved apricot jam on top of each, or a dollop of liqueur jam – there are many possibilities.

Sometimes for a real treat I make this yoghurt with $\frac{3}{4}$ pint of UHT milk and $\frac{1}{4}$ pint longlife cream. I use the longlife variety of milk and cream simply because I have found that these produce the best results.

Apricot Fool

$\frac{1}{2}$ lb. dried apricots	grated rind of 1 orange
$\frac{1}{2}$ pint thick yoghurt	sugar or honey to taste
small carton double cream, whipped	

Cover apricots with boiling water and soak overnight. Next day simmer until tender, then liquidise apricots with just sufficient water to make a thick purée. Add yoghurt, cream, half the orange rind, and sugar or honey to taste. Spoon into glasses and garnish with the rest of the grated orange rind.

Raspberry Fool

1 can raspberries or $\frac{1}{2}$ lb. fresh raspberries	$\frac{1}{2}$ pint yoghurt honey to taste

Strain syrup from raspberries, or wash fresh raspberries, then mix them well with the yoghurt and honey to taste if necessary. Serve chilled, with cream if liked.

Yoghurt and Orange Flip

$\frac{3}{4}$ glass fresh orange juice or
1 orange

2 heaped tbs. yoghurt
honey, cinnamon, nutmeg

A quick meal-in-a-glass. To $\frac{3}{4}$ glass of orange juice add 2 heaped tbs. of yoghurt. Stir well, or liquidise, add a pinch of cinnamon or nutmeg if liked, and also sweeten with honey to taste, if desired. Alternatively this can be made by liquidising a whole orange and 1 tbs. honey with two or three good heaped tbs. yoghurt, then straining into a glass.

FRUIT DESSERTS

Rosy Apples

4 medium-sized cooking apples
4 tbs. red currant jelly or apple and rosepetal jelly

2 wineglasses red wine
small carton double cream
4 tbs. toasted almonds

Peel and core apples and arrange in lightly buttered baking dish. Put a tablespoon of red currant jelly or rosepetal jelly into the centre of each apple. Pour red wine round apples. Cover with greased foil or lid and bake for about 45 minutes, in a moderate oven, 350 °F., gas mark 4, until apples are tender but not breaking. Whip cream, and at last minute pipe a good swirl into each apple cavity. Sprinkle with toasted almonds and serve at once. Delicious hot or cold.

Stuffed Apples

4 large apples	1 banana
a little lemon juice	2 tsp. clear honey
4 oz. black grapes	small carton double cream
1 orange	(optional)
	toasted flaked almonds

Halve apples around their middles. Cut out flesh to make apple 'cups'. Brush cups with lemon juice. Chop flesh. Halve grapes and remove pips; cut skin from orange and cut flesh into pieces; peel and slice banana. Mix all fruit together, add honey and spoon into apple 'cups'. Top with a good swirl of cream, if using, and scatter with toasted flaked almonds.

Real Apricot Jelly

4 oz. dried apricots	double cream, honey to taste,
boiling water to cover	dried apricot and angelica
2 level tsp. agar agar	to garnish

Soak apricots overnight in boiling water to cover. Next day cook until tender, then liquidise. Measure liquid and add water to make up to 1 pint if necessary. Reheat to boiling point, then sprinkle agar agar over, a little at a time, whisking between each addition. Cook gently for 2 minutes, sweeten, pour into bowls and leave to set. When cold, garnish with double cream, thin slices of dried apricot and angelica if using.

Bananas with Chocolate Sauce

4 ripe bananas	$\frac{1}{4}$ pint water
2 tbs. cocoa	$\frac{1}{2}$ oz. butter
1 tbs. brown sugar	2 tbs. top milk or single cream

Peel and slice bananas and divide between 4 bowls. To make sauce boil together cocoa, sugar and water for

5–10 minutes; add butter and top of milk or cream. Pour over bananas and serve immediately, with a little cream, if liked. If bananas have to wait for any length of time, toss them in lemon or orange juice to preserve their colour. Other fresh fruits, such as apples or pears can be used instead of bananas. A very popular sweet with children!

Melon and Orange Compôte

1 large ripe melon	2 tbs. clear honey
4 large oranges	a little orange liqueur, if liked

Dice melon or make into balls using a vegetable scoop; add oranges, skinned and cut into segments; mix with clear honey and a little orange liqueur if liked. Serve in individual glasses, or pile back into the melon skin, and serve on fresh green rose leaves. Skin can be vandyked around the edge if liked.

Melon and Orange Slices

1 ripe melon	1 level tsp. agar agar
$\frac{1}{2}$ pint orange juice	honey to taste
(approx. 4 large oranges)	

Cut the melon in half and remove seeds. Enlarge the hole in the centre of each half a little by scooping out some of the flesh neatly with a teaspoon – this flesh can be used up in a salad or fruit compôte. Heat the orange juice to boiling point, sprinkle on the agar agar a little at a time, stirring until dissolved. Remove from heat, sweeten with honey if necessary (don't make it too sweet) and pour into the melon halves. Leave in a cool place to set. Cut each half into two or three slices, depending on size; the resulting slices of melon topped with orange jelly look pretty served as they are on individual plates, or against a background of green leaves.

This is simple to make but looks pretty and unusual. It

can be made in advance and left in a cool place.

Variation
Melon and Raspberry Slices

Make as above, using a can of raspberries and 1 level tsp. of agar agar to every ½ pint of liquid and fruit measured together.

Muesli

1 rounded tbs. compost grown oat flakes	1 tbs. lemon juice a little grated lemon rind
1 tbs. sweetened condensed milk	4 oz. fruit – grated apple or soft fruit in season
3 tbs. cold water	1 tbs. milled nuts

Mix together the oat flakes, condensed milk, water, lemon juice and rind to a creamy consistency, then mix in the fruit. Serve sprinkled with nuts. If you find, as I do, that this mixture is a little sweet, the condensed milk and water can be omitted from the recipe, and 3 tbs. ordinary milk (or single cream) can be used instead, with honey to taste. The above quantities serve one person.

This is the original Bircher-Benner recipe for a perfect sweet or breakfast dish. Dr. Bircher-Benner originally invented it as a complete, nourishing, supper dish, and served it with thinly sliced wholemeal bread, honey and herb tea, in his famous clinic.

Orange Cups

4 large oranges	dash of orange liqueur (optional)
½ lb. black cherries or black grapes or strawberries	*to serve:* fresh non-poisonous green leaves, such as bayleaves or rose leaves; double cream; toasted almonds
a little honey to taste	

Slice about a quarter off the top of each orange, and, using a grapefruit knife, cut out all the flesh and chop, removing any tough pith. Mix the flesh with the cherries or other fruit used, honey and a little orange liqueur if using. Pile mixture back into orange 'cups' – it may be necessary to slice a little off the bottom of each so that they will stand level. If possible, serve the oranges on a bed of fresh, non-poisonous leaves, such as rose or bay-leaves, and if liked, top each with a generous whirl of cream and a scattering of toasted flaked almonds.

Real Orange Jelly

$\frac{1}{2}$ pint water	$\frac{1}{2}$ pint fresh orange juice
2 tbs. honey	1 tsp. lemon juice
2 level tsp. agar agar	

Heat the water and honey until boiling. Gradually sprinkle the agar agar into the liquid, stir until dissolved, and then remove from heat. Add the orange and lemon juice, mix well, pour into glasses and allow to set. Serve with cream.

A sliced banana or a sliced rosy eating apple is good added to this.

Orange Water Ice

$\frac{1}{2}$ pint water	juice of $\frac{1}{2}$ lemon
2 tbs. thick honey or	2 egg whites
4 oz. demerara sugar	shiny green leaves
4 large oranges	

Simmer together the water and honey or demerara sugar over a low heat for 10 minutes, then cool. Meanwhile, cut tops off oranges, and, using a grapefruit knife, scoop out flesh. Leave orange skins on one side; liquidise or sieve orange flesh, add the lemon juice and make up to $\frac{1}{2}$ pint with extra orange juice if necessary, then add the cooled syrup. Freeze until mixture begins to set around the edges, then beat thoroughly. Whisk egg whites until stiff and fold into the orange mixture. Refreeze until frozen but still soft. Spoon into orange-skin 'cups' and serve on a plate surrounded by non-poisonous leaves – bayleaves, if possible or a few rose leaves.

Peach and Raspberry Cream

4 large ripe peaches
juice of $\frac{1}{2}$ lemon
a little caster sugar
  or honey
8 oz. pkt. frozen
  raspberries, thawed

2 tbs. sweet white wine or a
  little kirsch (optional)
$\frac{1}{2}$ pint double cream
4 tbs. demerara sugar

Wipe peaches and slice finely; toss in lemon juice; scatter with sugar or mix with a little honey and leave for half-an-hour, then mix with the raspberries, wine or kirsch if using and put into a heat-proof dish – a heat-proof glass one is nice. Whip cream lightly and spread over fruit. Top with the demerara sugar and leave in fridge until ready to serve, then pop under a hot grill to melt the sugar.

The combination of ice-cold fruit, hot sugar, soft cream and crispy topping is delicious.

Stuffed Peaches

4 large peaches
small carton double
  cream

4 oz. fresh or frozen raspberries
  or fresh black grapes,
  de-seeded
1–2 tbs. kirsch (optional)

Blanch peaches by putting into boiling water; leave for 1 minute, then drain off water and cover with cold water. Remove skins. Halve peaches and remove stones. Whip cream, fold in raspberries (or grapes) and liqueur, if using. Heap into peach cavities and serve within an hour or so. A few flaked almonds can be scattered on top if liked.

Variations

Stuffed Apricots

Allow 3–4 halves per person and make as above.

Stuffed Pears

Make as above allowing 1 pear per person.

Chocolate Pear Pudding

2 eggs	2½ oz. real barbados
2 oz. caster sugar	chocolate, melted
2 oz. wholemeal flour	1 lb. dessert pears
	a few flaked almonds

Whisk together eggs and sugar at maximum speed in electric mixer until double in bulk and light in colour. If no mixer is available separate eggs and whisk whites till stiff but not dry. Beat in yolks and sugar. Sift flour and fold lightly into egg mixture together with any residue of bran left in sieve. Melt chocolate and fold into sponge mixture. Peel and thinly slice pears and put into shallow greased baking dish. Pour chocolate mixture on top; scatter with flaked almonds, and bake in a fairly hot oven, 400 °F., gas mark 6, for 30–40 minutes, until firm to the touch. Serve with single cream.

Pineapple and Grape Compôte

1 large ripe pineapple	2 tbs. clear honey
4 oz. white grapes	2 tbs. orange juice or
4 oz. black grapes	grand marnier
	whipped cream to serve
	(optional)

Remove prickly skin and top from pineapple. Cut flesh into neat dice, removing hard core. Halve grapes and remove pips. Arrange fruit in a large glass bowl, pour over honey and orange juice, or grand marnier, and turn once or twice to mix. Leave for at least 2 hours in a cool place. Serve as it is, or with whipped cream. The liqueur version is delicious for special occasions and makes this simple dessert into a gourmet one.

Real Pineapple Jelly

1 large can unsweetened pineapple juice
2 level tsp. agar agar
8 oz. can pineapple pieces
a few drops pineapple liqueur (optional)
double cream
angelica

Put the juice into a pan and bring to the boil, then gradually sprinkle the agar agar over the boiling liquid until dissolved. Remove from heat. Drain liquid from the pineapple pieces and rinse under cold water; divide between 4–6 glasses, sprinkle with a little pineapple liqueur if using. Pour the juice over the pineapple pieces and leave until set. Decorate with double cream and angelica.

As a change from the canned pineapple, try sliced banana or eating apple instead.

Red Fruit Dessert – Röd Gröd

½ lb. mixed fresh ripe red fruit, such as raspberries, red currants, strawberries
1 pint water
2 oz. cornflour
4 oz. caster sugar
a little lemon juice
sponge finger biscuits and cream and flaked almonds to serve

The fruit should be really ripe and fresh. Wash, then liquidise with the water and strain. Use a little of this purée to mix the cornflour to a smooth cream. Heat the rest, with the sugar, to boiling point, then add to the cornflour mixture and reheat, stirring until thickened. Taste, and add a little lemon juice or more sugar if necessary. Pour into glass dishes and cool. Serve, either really chilled, or, as I prefer, just warm, with a dollop of whipped cream and a scattering of flaked almonds. This version of Röd Gröd differs from the usual ones in that the fruit is used fresh, and not precooked. This preserves the fresh flavours. A very good recipe for making a little fruit go a long way.

Gateaux

Basic Swiss Roll Sponge

2 eggs	*filling:*
2 oz. caster sugar	2 heaped tbs. raspberry jam
2 oz. wholemeal flour	$\frac{1}{2}$ pint double cream
	icing sugar to dredge

Set oven at 425 °F., gas mark 7. If using an electric beater whisk together eggs and sugar at maximum speed until double in bulk and light in colour – 5 minutes. Otherwise separate eggs, whisk whites until stiff but not dry, then beat in yolks and sugar. Sift flour and fold in lightly, together with any residue of bran left in sieve. Spread mixture evenly into a lined swiss roll tin, bake in preheated oven for 8 minutes, until cake springs back when touched. Do not overbake. Turn out swiss roll and allow to cool, then strip off greaseproof paper, spread sponge with jam and whipped cream. Trim long edges with a sharp knife, make a cut across, $\frac{1}{2}''$ from one of the shorter edges of the cake and halfway into it, to make the first fold easier; fold this over and roll up firmly. Place on a serving dish and dredge with icing sugar. Swiss roll will roll up perfectly without cracking as long as sponge is not overbaked.

Alternatively swiss roll can be filled with $\frac{1}{2}$ lb. chopped fresh strawberries or other fresh soft fruit sweetened to taste with a little sugar, instead of the jam.

Peach Gateau

1 quantity of swiss roll mixture, as above	2 tbs. apricot jam, sieved
1 lb. 13 oz. can peach halves	1–2 heaped tbs. toasted flaked almonds
½ pint double cream	

Prepare and bake sponge exactly as for swiss roll; cool. Reserve 3 'best' peach halves; chop rest fairly finely. Cut the sponge across into 3 equal portions. Place one on a serving dish and spread with a quarter of the cream and half the chopped peaches. Place second piece of sponge on top of this, followed by another quarter of the cream and the rest of the chopped peaches. Top with the last piece of sponge; arrange the reserved peach halves on top of this. Brush peaches with the warmed sieved apricot jam. Coat the sides of the cake with half the remaining cream and press toasted almonds into the sides with a palette knife. Using a medium shell nozzle pipe the rest of the cream down each side of the peaches and decorate with a few toasted almonds.

The basic swiss roll mixture can also be used to make a sponge flan case:

Almond and Apricot Flan

1 quantity swiss roll, made as above	2 tbs. sieved apricot jam
1 lb. 13 oz. can apricots	½ pint double cream
	2 heaped tbs. toasted almonds

Make the swiss roll sponge as described on p. 172; turn mixture into a foil-lined and well-buttered 7″ sponge flan tin and bake in a moderately hot oven, 400 °F., gas mark 6, for 20 minutes. Turn out and allow to cool. Drain apricots and rinse under cold water to remove excess sweetness. Arrange apricots in flan. Heat sieved apricot jam in pan until melted, then pour evenly over apricots. Whip cream until stiff, spread half all around outside of flan case. Using a palette knife, pat toasted almonds on to this to coat. Put rest of cream into piping bag with shell nozzle and decorate top of flan.

Well-cooked dried apricots can replace canned if preferred. Soak dried apricots overnight, then cook until tender.

Black Forest Gateau

2 eggs	$\frac{1}{2}$ pint double cream
2 oz. caster sugar	2–3 tbs. kirsch
$1\frac{1}{2}$ oz. wholemeal flour	$\frac{1}{2}$ lb. black cherry jam
$\frac{1}{2}$ oz. cocoa	2 or 3 chocolate milk flakes

Set oven at 425 °F., gas mark 7. Line a swiss roll tin with greaseproof paper. Whisk together eggs and sugar at maximum speed on an electric mixer until double in bulk and light in colour – 5 minutes. If no mixer is available, separate eggs and whisk whites until stiff but not dry, then beat in yolks and sugar. Sift flour and cocoa, and fold lightly into egg mixture, together with any residue of bran left in sieve. Spread mixture evenly into lined tin and bake for 8 minutes until cake springs back when touched. Do not overbake. Turn out and allow to cool, then cut cake across into three equal oblongs. Sprinkle with half the kirsch. Whip cream stiffly and add half the kirsch, whip again, lightly. Place one piece of chocolate cake on a pretty serving plate. Spread with a third of the jam and a generous layer of cream. Place another piece of sponge on top, spread with jam and cream, and top with the final piece of sponge. Spread a little cream around the sides of the gateau and press crumbled chocolate flake into the cream. Spoon a narrow strip of jam lengthways across the top of the gateau, then using a large shell nozzle, pipe cream down each side of the jam. Decorate top with some pieces of chocolate flake.

Chocolate Pear Gateau

1 chocolate swiss roll sponge made as above	chopped walnuts or vermicelli
1 lb. 4 oz. can pears	redcurrant jelly
½ pint double cream	2 or 3 chocolate milk flakes

Make the sponge, bake and cut as described for Black Forest Gateau, p. 174. Reserve 3 pears; chop rest and layer with the cream, as for Black Forest Gateau. Smooth cream around the sides, and press chopped walnuts or vermicelli on to the cream. Place reserved pear halves on top, pour over the warmed redcurrant jelly, and using a shell nozzle, pipe the rest of the cream down sides. Decorate with crushed milk flake.

Gateau aux Marrons

8 oz. plain chocolate	4 oz. flaked almonds
2 tbs. milk	dash of rum
15½ oz. can unsweetened chestnut purée	small carton cream, whipped
	grated chocolate

Melt chocolate with milk in a pan over a gentle heat, then beat into the chestnut purée and add flaked almonds and rum to taste. Spread into a 7″ sandwich tin which has been lined with a circle of greaseproof. Place in fridge to firm up. To serve, turn out, pipe or spoon cream over the top and scatter generously with grated chocolate.

Basic Meringue Gateau

2 egg whites   4 oz. real demerara or caster sugar

Whisk egg whites until stiff and dry, then thoroughly beat in half the sugar to make a smooth, glossy mixture. Fold in remaining sugar. Draw two circles 6″ in diameter, on greaseproof, foil or silicone paper, and brush the greaseproof or foil with oil. Pipe or spoon meringue mixture to cover circles evenly. Alternatively, draw only one circle, then pipe circles of meringue round at sides to build up into a flan shape. Bake in a slow oven at 250 °F., gas mark $\frac{1}{2}$, for 2–3 hours, until crisp and dry but not brown. Cool. Peel off paper. Store in airtight tin until required for filling in any of the following ways:

Chestnut Meringue Gateau

$1\frac{1}{2}$ quantity meringue mixture
1 small can sweetened chestnut purée

$\frac{1}{2}$ pint double cream
dash of kirsch
chopped marron glacé or chocolate flake ⎫ (optional)

Use meringue mixture to make 3 circles exactly as described above. Slightly warm chestnut purée and beat well until smooth. Whip cream and kirsch together. Sandwich the meringue circles together with the chestnut mixture and three-quarters of the cream. Pipe the top decoratively with the remaining cream, and garnish with chopped marron glacé if available. Otherwise, scatter with chocolate flake.

Meringue Mountain

$1\frac{1}{2}$ quantity meringue mixture as above
$\frac{1}{2}$ pint double cream

crystallised rose and violet petals
angelica

Make up meringue mixture and pipe or spoon into small even-sized rounds on oiled foil-lined baking sheets. Bake as for meringue circles until crisp all through. Leave on baking sheets to cool. Store until ready to serve. Whip cream. Place a circle of the meringues on a flat serving dish, sticking them together with the cream. Top with a smaller circle, and build up to form a pyramid, with plenty of cream between all the gaps. This looks best piped on through a shell nozzle. Finish with a few swirls of cream here and there if any is left, and then decorate with crystallised rose petals, violet petals and thin strips of angelica cut to resemble leaves. Serve as soon as possible – not more than 2 hours after assembling.

Pineapple Meringue Flan

1 meringue flan case
  made as above
1 fresh pineapple
sugar to taste

½ pint double cream
a little kirsch (optional)
angelica or pistachio nuts
  to decorate

Peel, core, and dice pineapple; sweeten to taste. Whip cream and fold in pineapple and kirsch, if using. Pile into meringue flan case and decorate top with chopped angelica or pistachios.

Strawberry or Raspberry Meringue

½ lb. strawberries or
  raspberries, hulled
caster sugar

2 meringue circles, made
  as above
½ pint double cream

Sprinkle hulled strawberries or fresh raspberries with a little caster sugar; leave for at least 30 minutes. Spread one circle with half the cream, whipped, and half the fruit. Cover with second circle, and pipe circles of cream on top; decorate with remaining fruit. For special occasions strawberries or raspberries can be sprinkled with a little grand marnier.

Refrigerator Chocolate Cake

8 oz. unsalted butter
1 tbs. sugar
2 eggs, separated
8 oz. plain chocolate

2 tbs. sherry or rum (optional)
8 oz. semisweet biscuits,
  lightly crushed
small carton double cream
2 oz. flaked almonds

Cream together butter and sugar; when light and fluffy beat in the egg yolks. Melt chocolate and beat in with the sherry or rum if using, then add broken biscuits. Whip egg whites until stiff but not dry and fold into chocolate mixture. Line a square cake tin with foil and spoon in mixture. Smooth top and chill in fridge until firm. To serve, turn out of tin and spread with stiffly whipped cream. Scatter with the nuts.

This is a nice easy dessert for entertaining and parties and cuts well when firm.

SMALL CAKES AND BISCUITS

Brandy Snaps

4 oz. butter or margarine	1 small tsp. ground ginger
4 oz. light barbados sugar	a little grated lemon rind
4 oz. golden syrup	$\frac{1}{2}$ pint double cream
4 oz. plain flour	few drops brandy (optional)

Stir the butter, brown sugar and golden syrup together in a pan over a gentle heat until melted. Remove from heat and sift in the flour, ground ginger and a little grated lemon rind to taste. Drop teaspoonfuls of mixture on to greased baking sheets; flatten lightly with palette knife; leave plenty of room for them to spread. Bake in a moderate oven, 325 °F., gas mark 3, for 8–10 minutes, until golden. Cool slightly, then loosen with a knife and quickly roll snaps round the greased handle of a wooden spoon, then slide off and leave to cool. This process must be done quickly or the brandy snaps will harden. Should this happen, pop them back into the oven for a few minutes to soften. When quite cold use piping bag with star nozzle to fill the brandy snaps with whipped cream (flavoured with a touch of brandy if liked). Brandy snaps can be made a day or two in advance and stored in a tin ready for filling with cream when desired. Makes approximately 12.

Chocolate Shortbread

4 oz. margarine	2½ oz. desiccated coconut
2 oz. dark brown sugar	2 tbs. cocoa powder
3½ oz. plain flour	2 oz. plain chocolate

Cream together the margarine and sugar until well blended, then add flour, coconut and cocoa and mix well. Press mixture firmly into a greased swiss roll tin (a palette knife helps here) and bake in a moderate oven, 350 °F., gas mark 4, for 30 minutes. While shortbread is cooking, break chocolate into small pieces or grate coarsely. When shortbread is cooked, scatter chocolate over the top, and return shortbread to oven for a minute or two, until chocolate has melted. Remove from oven and spread chocolate evenly over top. Cool in tin, then cut into slices.

Flapjacks

6 oz. natural brown sugar	2 tbs. golden syrup
6 oz. margarine	8 oz. rolled oats

Melt together the brown sugar, margarine and golden syrup, then stir in the rolled oats. Spread into a greased swiss roll tin, and bake at 375 °F., gas mark 5, for 20 minutes until golden and crisp. Cool a little, then mark into slices. Remove from tin when quite cold.

Frosted Fingers

½ lb. suenut	2 cups rice crispies
1 cup coconut	2 oz. raisins
1 cup icing sugar	2 oz. glacé cherries
1 cup skimmed milk powder	

Melt, but do not overheat the suenut, then stir in the coconut, skimmed milk powder, icing sugar, rice crispies and raisins. Spread into a swiss roll tin, smooth over top and decorate with cherries. Allow to cool but slice into fingers before quite cold and firm.

This is a quick and useful recipe which can be varied ad infinitum; try adding nuts, or chocolate polka dots, more or less dried fruit. Can also be covered with a layer of melted chocolate when quite cold.

Quick Easy Florentines

8 oz. plain chocolate	3 heaped tbs. chopped nuts
2 oz. margarine	2 heaped tbs. glacé cherries
4 oz. soft brown sugar	2 heaped tbs. mixed peel
1 egg	2 heaped tbs. sultanas
5 heaped tbs. desiccated coconut	

Melt chocolate and spread in the bottom of a swiss roll tin; leave to set. Beat together the margarine and sugar, add egg and then the other ingredients. Spread mixture over chocolate and bake in a slow oven, 325 °F., gas mark 3, for 30–40 minutes until set and golden. Leave to cool, then cut into slices or use a plain round pastry cutter to make circles.

Florentines are delectable, but such a bore to make by the normal, fiddly method. So I've evolved this simple way. You make them completely in a swiss roll tin, then cut them up with a round pastry cutter. The odd-shaped bits can be cut into little petit fours – if the children don't get them first!

Macaroons

6 oz. ground almonds	a drop of orange flower
8 oz. demerara sugar	water (optional)
2 tbs. ground rice	blanched almonds
2 egg whites	rice paper

Blend together all ingredients except for blanched almonds, and beat well. Put teaspoonfuls of the mixture on to rice paper, and for a shiny finish smooth over with a palette knife dipped in cold water. Lightly press blanched almond on top of each. Bake in a slow oven, 300 °F., gas mark 2, for 20–30 minutes. Cool, then using kitchen scissors cut neatly round each macaroon.

Pastries and Tarts

It is no good pretending that wholemeal flour has the same texture as white; it hasn't. It is not as glutinous, and this is never more noticeable than when making pastry, which has a much more crumbly texture when made with wholemeal flour. However, when properly made, wholemeal pastry has a delicious flavour and should have a melt-in-the-mouth texture as well; though, like the proverbial nut cutlet, wholemeal pastry badly made can be solemn to a degree. However, let's steer clear of such miseries with the following recipes.

The flour used in these is 100 per cent plain wholemeal, Allinsons', Prewett's or Sam Mayall's. If you find difficulty in adjusting to the texture of wholemeal flour you might like to mix it in equal proportions with 81 per cent at first.

Wholemeal Shortcrust

8 oz. plain flour	2 oz. vegetable fat
2 level tsp. baking powder	2 oz. vegetable margarine
$\frac{1}{2}$ tsp. salt	2 tbs. cold water

Sift together flour, baking powder and salt. There will be a residue of bran left in the sieve – add this to the sifted flour. Rub in fats until mixture looks like fine breadcrumbs, then add water and gather pastry together. Roll out in the ordinary way on a floured board, taking extra care as mixture will be more crumbly than that made with white flour. Use as required.

Cottage Cheese Pastry

8 oz. plain flour
2 level tsp. baking powder
$\frac{1}{2}$ tsp. salt
4 oz. soft butter or margarine

4 oz. cottage cheese, curd cheese or cream cheese
1–2 tsp. lemon juice
a little cold water

Sift flour, baking powder and salt, as in previous recipe. Rub in butter or margarine and when mixture resembles fine breadcrumbs add cottage, curd or cream cheese, lemon juice and a little cold water, if required, to make dough. Roll out, fold into three like an envelope, half turn and roll out again. Use as required, chilling first for an hour or so if possible. This is a useful pastry as it gives extra protein. It is also light and flaky.

Bakewell Tart

6 oz. shortcrust pastry
4 oz. soft margarine or butter
4 oz. light brown sugar
2 eggs

few drops almond essence
1 oz. plain flour
2 oz. ground almonds
3 tbs. raspberry jam or Marigold damson jam
a few flaked almonds

Use pastry to line 7″ ovenproof flan dish. Cream margarine or butter and sugar together until light and fluffy; gradually beat in eggs and a drop of almond essence. Fold in flour and ground almonds. Cover base of pastry with jam, spread with almond mixture and sprinkle with a few flaked almonds. Bake in a hot oven, 425 °F., gas mark 7, for 5 minutes, then turn the heat down to moderate, 350 °F., gas mark 4, and bake for a further 30–35 minutes, until golden and firm to the touch. Serve hot with single cream, or cold, in slices. This of course is the classic, but do try

Variation

Chocolate Cherry Bakewell

This is made as above, but using 3 tbs. black cherry jam instead of the raspberry jam, and adding 2 tsp. cocoa powder and a little milk if necessary, to the sponge filling.

Christmas Pie

6 oz. shortcrust pastry
½ small fresh pineapple,
  peeled, cored and diced

4 tbs. mincemeat
beaten egg, or milk
  to glaze

Use two-thirds of the pastry to line a shallow dish or pie plate. Mix together the pineapple and mincemeat and spread over pastry. Damp edges with cold water and top with the rest of the pastry, rolled out to fit; prick; brush with beaten egg or milk, and bake in a hot oven, 425 °F., gas mark 7, for 20 minutes. Serve hot or cold, dredged with caster sugar.

Variation

Use 1 lb. cooking apples, peeled and finely sliced, instead of pineapple. In this case a little extra sugar may be needed.

Strawberry Flan

6 oz. digestive biscuits
3 oz. melted butter or
  margarine
small carton double cream
4 oz. cottage or cream
  cheese

½–¾ lb. strawberries
4 tbs. Marigold apple
  and rosepetal jelly or
  red currant jelly

Make biscuit crust by crushing biscuits between 2 pieces of greaseproof paper with a rolling pin, then mixing with the melted butter or margarine. Press mixture into a loose-bottomed flan tin and leave in a cool place to firm up. Meanwhile make filling; whip cream until thick; sieve cottage cheese or beat cream cheese with a fork until smooth, then lightly mix the cheese with the whipped cream. Spread over base of flan and smooth top. The filling can be put into flan before it has fully set, and then the whole thing left in a cold place for at least 2 hours. Carefully wash and hull strawberries, halving large ones and arrange on top of cream. Melt jelly in a saucepan and pour over the berries.

Variations

Apricot Flan

Use a large can of apricots, well drained and rinsed in cold water to remove excess sweetness. Glaze with sieved apricot jam.

Blackberry Flan

Use ½ lb. ripe, sweet blackberries; glaze with blackcurrant jelly or bramble jelly.

Cherry Flan

Is made by using black cherry jam on top of cottage cheese. I like to add 1–2 tbs. kirsch to the jam first.

Grape Flan

Using ½ lb. black and white grapes mixed. Halve, and remove stones; glaze with sieved apricot jam.

Peach Flan

Is lovely in the summer. Made by using 3 or 4 ripe peaches, prepared as for apricots, and glazed with Marigold rosepetal jelly or redcurrant jelly.

Raspberry Flan

Is prepared as for Strawberry Flan, glazing with a red jelly, as above.

Uncooked Lemon Cheese Cake

6 oz. digestive biscuits	6 tbs. lemon curd
3 oz. butter	$\frac{1}{4}$ pint double cream
8 oz. carton cottage cheese	

Crush digestive biscuits between 2 pieces of greaseproof paper with rolling pin. Melt butter and mix with biscuit crumbs. Press into fluted flan tin or flan ring on a flat dish; leave in a cool place to become firm. Meanwhile sieve cottage cheese, beat in 4 tbs. lemon curd and fold in the cream. Smooth into prepared flan and leave to set. Glaze top by spreading with rest of lemon curd, slightly warmed if necessary, before serving.

BREADS

Wholemeal flour may not be as easy to use as white flour in some ways, but, whatever its shortcomings with pastry and cakes, it does enable one to make a really good quick yeast loaf! The one stage yeast loaf (the Grant loaf) is now very well known: I hope I'll be forgiven for giving yet another version of it in an effort to encourage more people to experience the delights of fragrant, freshly-baked home-made bread. It's all so much easier than many people realise: somehow bread-making has acquired a quite unnecessary reverence and mystique; let's dispel it.

Any 100 per cent wholemeal flour can be used, but I prefer Allinsons' or Sam Mayall's for bread-making.

Quick Yeast Bread

½ pint boiling water	1 tbs. salt
1 pint cold water	3 lbs. Allinsons'
2 tbs. dried yeast	wholemeal flour
2 tbs. dark barbados sugar	1 oz. fat

Mix together the boiling water and the cold water,
Place a third of the water into a bowl and sprinkle in the
yeast and 1 tsp. of the sugar. Leave for 5 minutes to
'froth up'. Meanwhile sift the flour and salt and rub in
the fat. Make a well in the centre and pour in yeast
mixture and rest of water; mix until dough forms, then
knead for 5 minutes – dough hooks on an electric mixer
make light work of this job. Divide dough into four equal
pieces and shape each to fit a 1 lb. buttered bread tin.
Cover with teacloth or greased polythene and leave in a
warm place until risen 1″ above tops of tins – about 45
minutes. Bake in a fairly hot oven, 400 °F., gas mark 6,
for 30–35 minutes, until bottom of loaf removed from
tin and tapped sounds hollow. Tops of loaves can be
sprinkled with crushed wheat, or glazed with beaten egg,
before baking to give a good finish.

Variations

Crisp Rolls

Divide dough into four as before, but divide one of
these quarters into eight pieces, roll in flour and leave on
a greased baking sheet or bun tin till double its size. Bake
for 10 minutes.

Soft Rolls

Use one quarter of above dough and add one egg and
1 oz. melted butter. Roll in flour and shape into 8
rounds. Set to rise and bake as for rolls.

Hot Cross Buns

As for soft rolls, but with the inclusion of 1 tbs. sugar,
2 oz. currants, 1 oz. peel, ½ tsp. mixed spice. Mark with

cross using knife or make pastry cross or rice paper cross. When cooked brush immediately with glaze made by boiling 1 oz. demerara sugar in 1 tbs. milk until sugar is dissolved and mixture creamy looking.

And lastly a well known but delicious non-yeast bread.

Banana Bread

8 oz. wholemeal flour	3 oz. golden syrup or
2 level tsp. baking powder	honey
pinch salt	2 oz. walnuts
2 oz. margarine	1 egg
2 oz. dark barbados sugar	2 bananas

Sift together flour, baking powder and salt. Melt together margarine, sugar and syrup in a pan over a gentle heat. Chop walnuts; beat egg, mash bananas. Make a well in the centre of the flour and pour in margarine mixture; mix quickly, then add beaten egg and mashed bananas. Mix very well; pour into greased and lined 1 lb. loaf tin, and bake in a moderate oven, 350 °F., gas mark 4, for 1 hour.

Variation

Date and Walnut Loaf

Is made in the same way, using 4 oz. chopped dates and perhaps a little milk instead of bananas.

ICINGS, FILLINGS AND TOPPINGS

Properly speaking, icing sugar has no place in a strictly food reform diet, for there really is no 'wholefood' equivalent and I try to use it as little as possible. A very good, white american frosting can be made from real demerara sugar, and this can often take the place of glacé icing and royal icing. For chocolate cakes, melted barbados sugar chocolate makes an excellent icing, and butter icing can be made using the light brown barbados sugar, or demerara sugar which has been powdered in the liquidiser. Barbados sugar can also be used to make a special butter icing, below. Raw sugar jams and jellies also make good fillings, and toppings, too, if coated with flaked almond, desiccated coconut or grated raw sugar chocolate. Powdered demerara sugar is also good for sprinkling over the top of cakes for a quick, simple topping.

American Frosting

8 oz. real demerara sugar	pinch salt
2 tbs. water	2 egg whites
pinch of cream of tartar	

Place sugar, water, cream of tartar, salt and egg whites in bowl over gently boiling water. Stir with wooden spoon until sugar has dissolved. Whisk until frosting is thick – takes about 8 minutes by hand, 5 minutes with an electric whisk. Remove from heat; continue to whisk until frosting has cooled a little. Use at once.

Special Butter Icing

1 large egg yolk	4 oz. unsalted butter
3 tbs. light brown sugar	drop of vanilla essence
4 tbs. milk	

Whisk the egg yolk with the sugar until pale and fluffy. Bring the milk to the boil and whisk into the egg yolk and sugar; return to the pan and stir over a gentle heat until thickened. Leave until cold. Beat butter until light and fluffy, then gradually beat in the cold custard mixture; flavour with vanilla as required.

This is a useful butter icing as it can be made with unrefined sugar and still looks and tastes delicious.

Variations

Chocolate Butter Icing

Add 2 oz. melted chocolate to the butter, gradually, before adding the custard mixture.

Coffee Butter Icing

Dissolve 1 desstsp. instant coffee in the milk before pouring it over the yolk.

Cream

Fresh whipped cream makes the simplest and one of the best fillings and toppings for cakes. Cream can be sweetened, and flavoured with cocoa dissolved in hot water, or coffee essence, brandy, sherry or vanilla essence. Cake can be decorated with fresh or crystallised fruit, grated chocolate, etc.

Chocolate

Melted chocolate, poured over cake, is another very simple and effective topping.

Fudge Icing

2 oz. butter	8 oz. icing sugar
2 tbs. milk	coffee essence or cocoa to taste

Melt 2 oz. butter and 2 tbs. milk in a pan. Remove from heat and beat in 8 oz. icing sugar and coffee essence or cocoa to taste. Use at once as this icing sets quickly.

Glacé Fruit Topping

An effective topping for a fruit cake or plain cake can be made by first brushing top of cake with warm sieved apricot jam, then arranging a selection of glacé fruits on top. Use as colourful a selection as possible; red, green and yellow cherries, glacé pineapple and angelica. Wash fruit under hot water to remove excess sugar. Finish by brushing with more hot sieved apricot jam.

Glacé Icing

8 oz. sieved icing sugar   2 tbs. hot water

Mix well until well blended. Can be flavoured with coffee – add 2 tsp. instant coffee dissolved in the hot water. Or chocolate: replace 1 tbs. icing sugar with 1 tbs. cocoa. Or orange: use hot orange juice to mix instead of water.

Jam Topping

Sieved jam, or jelly, heated, makes good toppings for cakes. Pour over the hot jam, then finish with a good sprinkling of coarse desiccated coconut, or flaked almonds, or grated chocolate or crumbled milk flake.

Mocha Topping

Break 1 bar of real barbados chocolate into a small bowl; add 1 tbs. of coffee essence or strong black coffee and heat over a pan of hot water until melted. Pour over cake.

Sugar Topping

The simplest topping of all: a dredge of icing sugar or caster sugar. Or, for a fruit cake, roughly crush lump sugar and sprinkle over top of cake, with a few flaked almonds, before baking.

CAKE DECORATION

With the limited time most of us have, a bold speedy effect is all-important. Good bases for decoration are:

1. Stand the cake on a rack with a plate strategically placed underneath, and simply pour a plain layer of glacé icing or american frosting over it.

2. Butter icing or fudge icing, swirled round and round, with the tip of a round-ended knife.

3. As above, but instead of a swirl, make up and down wavy lines.

4. The above two methods, using the prongs of a fork to give a slightly different result.

5. Prongs of fork drawn in lines across and then downwards.

6. Icing sugar, sieved over at random, or, if preferred, a d'oyley, paper or plastic, can be placed over top of cake first. When icing has been sieved and d'oyley lifted, pattern will remain. A child's stencil can be used similarly, with good effect.

On these bases any decorations can be placed to tone with flavour of cake and colour of icing used. It is helpful to keep a supply of the following handy:

Angelica: useful chopped small and scattered, or just sliced thinly, then cut into diamonds or leaf shapes, using kitchen scissors. Angelica is easy to work with if just rinsed in warm water to remove sugar crystals and soften.

Chocolate flakes: very useful and quick, crushed and sprinkled.

Chocolate, grated: ditto.

Chocolate vermicelli: try to get the real dark vermicelli, not the pallid version. Useful scattered; a 1–2″ border of vermicelli round the top of a chocolate cake, and a smaller heap in the centre, looks effective, with or without walnuts, hazelnuts, or bits of milk flake as well.

Crystallised flowers: rose petals, mimosa and violets are all pretty. Mimosa flowers and angelica leaves look very effective round the edge of a cake iced with pale yellow glacé icing. For a pretty topping to a plain sponge, flavour glacé icing with rose essence, colour pale pink, and decorate with crystallised rose petals and angelica leaves. Violet flavour can similarly be added to glacé icing.

Crystallised fruits: ginger, pineapple and whole peel are good topping white glacé icing on ginger cakes, spice cakes or simple fruit cakes.

Glacé cherries: red, yellow and green, if you can get them – wash off syrup first under warm water.

Nuts: blanched almonds, flaked almonds, walnuts and hazelnuts are all useful. Use flaked almonds as they are, or toast them by placing for a few minutes in a moderate oven on a dry baking tin. Cool, and keep in a screw top jar. Use walnuts both whole and chopped; the latter make a good border for a coffee cake. Prepare hazelnuts by spreading out well on a dry baking sheet and popping in moderate oven for 20–30 minutes. Rub off skins in a clean teacloth or kitchen paper. Cool and store in a jar.

Orange and lemon rind: pretty grated on top of glacé iced cakes.

Sugar strands: coloured sugar strands make a quick and effective decoration scattered over the top of a glacé iced or butter iced cake, when there's no time for anything else!

WHERE TO BUY...

agar agar: the vegetable gelatine, from health shops

apple and rosepetal jelly: by Marigold Foods, Ltd., 29 Bell Street, London, N.W.1, from health shops

artichoke hearts: canned, from supermarkets and delicatessen

bamboo shoots: canned, from supermarkets, delicatessen and oriental food shops

barbados chocolate: Barbachoc, from health shops

basil chutney: by Marigold, from health shops

bean sprouts: if you're lucky and live near an oriental provision shop, you'll be able to get them fresh; otherwise, canned

black olives: cheapest to buy them loose from supermarkets

brewers' yeast: from health shops

bulgarian yoghurt: from health shops

cardamoms: see garam masala

chestnuts, canned whole:
chestnut purée: } supermarkets, health shops, delicatessen

chestnuts, dehydrated: health shops

cider vinegar:
wine vinegar: } supermarkets, health shops, good grocers

creamed coconut: by Mapletons, health shops

damson jam: by Marigold, health shops

dill pickle: delicatessen, good grocers, supermarkets

free range eggs: health shops and some grocers. For further details of where to buy free range eggs and incidentally organic products generally, see the *Organic Food Finder and Directory*, Rodale Press, Berkhamsted, Herts. 70p

garam masala: ⎫
ground cumin: ⎪ try health shops, delicatessen, Indian
ground coriander: ⎬ provision shops, or write to:
ground turmeric: ⎭ The Bombay Emporium,
70 Grafton Way,
London, W.1

Marigold vegetarian meat: from health shops

nuts: flaked almonds and walnuts, just about anywhere; other nuts, from health shops and most good grocers

nuttolene: by Granose, health shops

okra: canned, from health shops and delicatessen

plant milk: by Plamil, from health shops

protoveg: obtainable – either 'mince' or 'chunky' – in various flavours from health shops, or send for mail order form and full details to:

> Direct Foods Ltd.,
> Compassion in World Farming,
> Greatham, Liss, Hants.

Direct Foods, incidentally, acts as marketing agent for that very worthwhile charity, Compassion in World Farming, dedicated to the replacement of animal machines with direct-from-the-crop foods. Profits from sales of these 'direct foods' are recycled to provide more foods and sponsor research into ways of feeding the hungry nations

soy sauce: supermarkets, good grocers, health shops

stem ginger: usually in pretty bottle or jar, from supermarkets, good grocers

tabasco: supermarkets, delicatessen

tartex vegetable pâté: ⎫ by Mapletons, health shops and
tartex savoury roll: ⎭ increasingly, supermarkets

vine leaves: usually, they'll have to be canned, from delicatessen, unless you live near a delicatessen which sells them fresh

white mustard seed: see under garam masala

wholemeal flour: Allinsons' 100 per cent is easy to get almost anywhere and is the best for bread; my favourite for cakes and pastry, Mapletons', is not so widely available, but you should be able to get it from health shops. Allinsons' 81 per cent which I like to use to thicken sauces and some soups, is obtainable at health shops.

DEAR AMERICAN READER . . .

I hope and believe that you'll be able to adapt the recipes in this book according to your cup measurements and the ingredients available. To help you, I've compiled this list of equivalent ingredients and measurements, with the help of an American friend.

First, a little English/American dictionary:

English	*American*
aubergine	egg plant
cornflour	cornstarch
courgette	zucchini
demerara sugar	my friend says you don't have this (which I find hard to believe): it's a golden crystal sugar. Use caster or soft brown sugar instead
grill	broiler
Marigold	
vegetarian meat	see protoveg
marmite	it's a yeast extract: use savita
marrow	squash, or a very large zucchini, if ever they come that way
nuttolene	nuteena or protose
pinekernels	pignolias
protoveg	apparently you don't have this! It's dehydrated textured soya protein. I suggest you use a canned soya protein. Use double the quantity given in the recipe, and of course no need to worry about hydrating it. (You might like to marinade it in a little wine, though, for the sake of flavour.)
smoky snaps	'bacon bits'
spring onions	scallions

suenut   this is a hard, white vegetable fat (the vegetarian equivalent of suet). If you can't get it, you might like to use creamed coconut instead . . . if you can't get that, well, better forget it (it only comes in one recipe, actually, but it's a nice one)

vitpro   see note for protoveg

Now for measurements:

1 English pint	=	$2\frac{1}{2}$ cups
small carton cream or yoghurt	=	$\frac{1}{2}$ cup
1 oz. chopped or flaked nuts	=	2 tbs.
1 oz. cocoa or cornflour	=	3 tbs.
1 oz. fat, butter or margarine	=	2 tbs.
1 oz. flour	=	2 tbs.
1 oz. grated cheese	=	4 tbs.
1 oz. sugar, caster	=	2 tbs.
1 oz. sugar, dark brown	=	1 tbs.
1 lb. breadcrumbs, fresh	=	5 cups
1 lb. butterbeans	=	3 cups
1 lb. cottage or cream cheese	=	2 cups
1 lb. dried apricots, prunes, dates, sultanas, raisins	=	4 cups
1 lb. fat, butter or margarine	=	2 cups
1 lb. grated cheese	=	4 cups
1 lb. ground almonds, finely milled nuts	=	4 cups
1 lb. lentils, soya beans	=	2 cups
1 lb. macaroni	=	3 cups
1 lb. mashed potato	=	2 cups
1 lb. nuts, whole	=	4 cups
1 lb. rice, cooked or uncooked	=	2 cups
1 lb. rolled oats	=	3 cups
1 lb. semolina	=	2 cups
1 lb. sugar, dark brown	=	2 cups
1 lb. sugar, icing or caster	=	3 cups
1 lb. wholemeal flour	=	3 cups

NOTE ON METRICATION

Most recipes in this book will convert easily to metric measurements. To do this, here are the approximate metric equivalents of the units used:

1 lb. is roughly equivalent to $\frac{1}{2}$ kilo;
$\frac{1}{2}$ lb. is roughly equivalent to $\frac{1}{4}$ kilo or 250 grammes.

For smaller measurements, I think it is easiest to take:

1 oz. as being roughly equivalent to 25 grammes. For larger amounts, of up to $\frac{1}{2}$ lb., the 25 g. unit is easily multiplied, e.g. 2 oz. becomes 50 g., 6 oz. becomes 150 g. It must be emphasised that this is only approximate, but for the recipes in this book, except the cakes, it is usually accurate enough.

For liquid measurements:

1 pint is roughly equivalent to $\frac{1}{2}$ litre; the following other rough measurements can be used for smaller amounts:

$\frac{1}{2}$ pint is roughly equivalent to 250 millilitres;
$\frac{1}{4}$ pint is roughly equivalent to 125 millilitres.

The Celcius oven temperatures are also gradually being introduced. Here is a table of equivalents:

	°Fahrenheit	°Celcius	Gas Mark
Cool	200	93	$\frac{1}{4}$
	225	107	
Slow	250	121	$\frac{1}{2}$
	275	135	1
	300	149	2
Moderate	325	163	3
	350	177	4

Fairly hot	375	190		5
	400	204		6
Hot	425	218		7
	450	232		8
Very hot	475	246		9
	500	260		

INDEX MENU-PLANNER

It's not the cooking which takes the time but the thinking *what* to cook . . . so I've made this index as full as possible, as an aid to planning. I've listed salads under seasons as well as alphabetically, and also listed those which are complete in themselves as far as protein is concerned. Salads which make good starters I've also noted, under hors d'oeuvres. And for really busy days, I've listed speedy savouries under 'quick savouries, family' and 'quick savouries, entertaining' – for those occasions when it's a case of 'guess who's coming to dinner, Mummy'. I hope you find this helpful.

Part I General Index

Part II Planning

Comprising:

*quick if canned butterbeans or soya beans are used

*yoghurt version   †with suggested dressings

*but go easy on the oil/sauce/cream